LEAN AND GREEN
COOKBOOK FOR BEGINNERS

1500-Day Lean and Green & Fueling Hacks Recipes to Help You Manage Figure and Keep Healthy with 5 & 1 | 4 & 2 & 1 Meal Plans

Candace Ragan

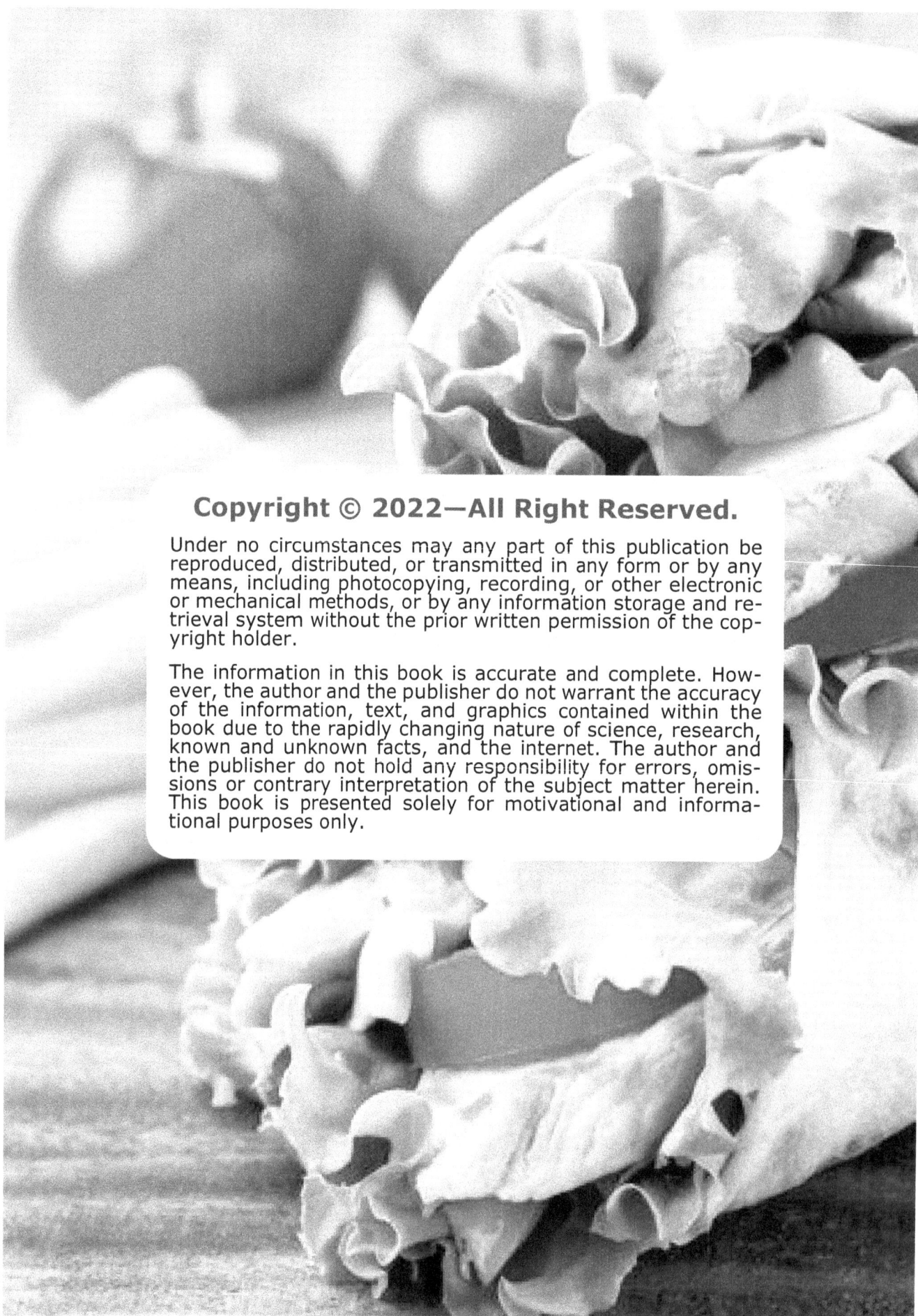

Copyright © 2022—All Right Reserved.

Under no circumstances may any part of this publication be reproduced, distributed, or transmitted in any form or by any means, including photocopying, recording, or other electronic or mechanical methods, or by any information storage and retrieval system without the prior written permission of the copyright holder.

The information in this book is accurate and complete. However, the author and the publisher do not warrant the accuracy of the information, text, and graphics contained within the book due to the rapidly changing nature of science, research, known and unknown facts, and the internet. The author and the publisher do not hold any responsibility for errors, omissions or contrary interpretation of the subject matter herein. This book is presented solely for motivational and informational purposes only.

Table of Contents

Introduction 7
    What is the Lean and Green Diet? 7
    Basic Plans of Lean and Green Diet 8
    Advantages of Lean and Green diet 8
    What can eat? 9
    What not to eat 9

Meal Plan 5 & 1 10
    Week 1 10
    Week-2 11
    Week-3 12
    Week-4 13

Meal Plan 4 & 2 & 1 14
    Week 1 14
    Week 2 15
    Week 3 16
    Week 4 17

Chapter 1 Breakfast Recipes 18
    Egg Broccoli Bread 18
    Blueberry Pancakes 18
    Oat Breads with Bananas 19
    Bacon and Brussels Sprout Meal 19
    Pumpkin Waffles 20
    Strawberry Yogurt Meal 20
    Spinach Waffles 21
    Eggs Avocado Toast 21
    Spinach Egg Bread 22
    Granola with Persimmon 22
    Coffee Banana Bread 23
    Chicken Avocado Salad 23
    Breakfast Donuts 24
    Cheesy Bacon Meal 24
    Zucchini Walnut Muffins 25
    Millet Coconut Porridge 25
    Pumpkin Banana Quinoa 26
    Squash Hash 26
    Mango Oatmeal 27
    Ricotta Egg Cups 27
    Quinoa Blueberry Porridge 28
    Barley Coconut Porridge 28

Chapter 2 Poultry Recipes 29
    Chicken and Red Cabbage Stew 29
    Lemon Chicken Thighs 29
    Jerk Chicken Drumettes 30

Chicken Cubes and Red Chard 30
Chicken Wontons 31
Turmeric Chicken Fillets 31
Chicken Mushroom Kabobs 32
Juicy Chicken Breast 32
Balsamic Chicken 33
Buffalo Chicken Meatballs 33
Crackling Chicken Breast 34
Creamy Cheese Chicken 34
Homemade Chicken Meatballs 35
Lemony Chicken Fillets 35
Broccoli Ranch Chicken 36
Baked Chicken Breasts 36
Simple Oregano Chicken Strips 37
Chicken Greens Salad 37
Chicken Strips with Capers 38
Almond Chicken Fillets 38
Chicken Breast and Mango 39
Mustard Parmesan Turkey Breast 39

Chapter 3 Red Meat Recipes 40

Sautéed Lean Beef Steak with Onions 40
Mediterranean Beef and Rice 40
Rosemary Steak with Kale 41
Beef Broccoli 41
Pork Broccoli Fry 42
Italian Lean Beef Meatballs 42
Beef Chili 43
Colombian Lean Beef Sirloin Steaks 43
Garlicky Pork Tenderloin 44
Beef with Mushrooms 44
Sirloin Steak with Broccoli 45
Ground Beef Fry 45
Beef Taco Meal 46
Juicy Steak 46
Veggie Stuffed Steak 47
Lean Beef and Eggplant 47
Beef Tenderloin Fillets and Mushrooms 48
Lean Lamb Burgers 48
Sirloin Steaks with Green Beans 49
Coffee Lean Skirt Steaks 49
Steak with Green Beans 50
Garlicky Lean Pork Ribs 50
Pork Veggie Burgers 51
Coriander Lean Lamb Chops 51
Pork Burgers 52

Chapter 4 Fish and Seafood Recipes 53

Lettuce Seafood Wraps 53
Mango Tilapia Fillets 53

Cod and Egg Sandwiches ... 54
Grilled Shrimp ... 54
Indian Spiced Cod ... 54
Thyme Shrimp ... 55
Shrimp Mix ... 55
Limey Trout Fillets ... 55
Fish Chili with Lentils ... 56
Tuna Casserole ... 56
Lemon Cod Fillets ... 57
Fish Soup ... 57
Chili Mussels with Parsley ... 58
Fried Scallops in Cream ... 58
Tuna Mushroom Casserole ... 59
Poached Halibut ... 59
Italian Sea Bass ... 60
Shrimp with Snow Peas ... 60
Lemon Rosemary Salmon ... 61
Lemon-Pepper Salmon ... 61
Salsa Shrimp ... 62
Turmeric Tuna Steaks ... 62
Salmon with Almonds ... 63
Limey Scallops ... 63
Roasted Cod with Capers ... 64
Shrimps Skewers ... 64

Chapter 5 Vegetarian Recipes ... 65

Tasty Cabbage Stew ... 65
Baked Cheese and Potato with Olives ... 65
Coconut Eggplant Curry ... 66
Baked Eggs with Spinach ... 66
Zucchini Sushi Rolls ... 67
Cheddar Broccoli Waffles ... 67
Mexican Baked Zucchini ... 68
Baked Eggs in Avocado Halves ... 68
Stuffed Banana Pepper ... 69
Creamy Spinach Waffles ... 69
Guacamole Deviled Eggs ... 70
Vegan Pesto ... 70
Cauldron Chicken Curry ... 71
Pumpkin and Kale with Polenta ... 72
Coleslaw with Barberries ... 73
Balsamic Arugula Lentil Salad ... 74
Cashew Leek Soup with Potato ... 75
Vegan Pad Thai ... 76
Broccoli Pesto Pasta ... 77
Zuppa Toscana ... 78
Corn Chowder ... 79

Chapter 6 Snack Recipes ... 80

Mayo Onion and Cauliflower Dip ... 80

Basil Pesto Crackers 80
Zucchini Taco Boats... 81
Creamy Kiwi Smoothie 81
Cashew Milk 82
Orange Juice Soda... 82
Oat Milk... 82
Creamy Caramel Cones 83
Stuffed Eggs... 83
Pumpkin Spiced Donuts 84
Roasted Seeds... 84
Asian Noodle Salad.. 85
Cinnamon Bites.. 85
Vegan Marinara.. 86
Pumpkin Muffins 86
Coconut Fat Bombs 87
Tomato Avocado Salad.. 87
Almond Chocolate Bites... 88
Watermelon Lemonade 88

Chapter 7 Dessert Recipes 89

Rhubarb Delight... 89
Lemony Raspberry Compote 89
Banana Bread.. 90
Custard Filled Pears.. 90
Lime Poached Pears... 91
Cinnamon Banana Cake 91
Creamy Cheesecake 92
Cherry Bread Pudding 92
Dark Chocolate Cherry Cookies 93
Banana Cake 93
Mini Lava Cakes 94
Apple Bread 94
Bread Dough in Amaretto 95
Cherry Cream 95
Bread Cherry Pudding 96
Cinnamon-flavored Wrapped Pears 96
Crusted Bananas 97
Minty Yogurt.. 97
Chocolate Peanut Butter Cups 98
Chocolate Fondue 98

Conclusion... 99

Appendix Measurement Conversion Chart.. 100

Introduction

Research has shown that eating a green diet is more beneficial than eating an average diet. Lean and Green Diet will help you lower your cholesterol levels and reduce inflammation. Moreover, it may help you shed a few inches off your waist. You can experience these benefits by adding more greens to your meal plans.

What is the Lean and Green Diet?

The diet includes five to seven ounces of cooked lean protein and three servings of non-starchy vegetables or legumes such as beans. It focuses on providing clean energy to the body with high protein and low carbs.

Besides, eating a plant-based diet is not only good for your health, but it's also good for the environment. The gist of this diet is to focus on eating mostly whole foods in their natural form while also trying not to waste any food.

You can take up a diet containing fuelings and lean & green meals spread over two plans focusing on weight loss and maintenance, respectively. There are several other meal replacement diet plans, but only some features set leafy green dietary practices.

Basic Plans of Lean and Green Diet

A diet full of greens also supports your nutrient intake requirements. You can start by including low-calorie meals in your diet. Here are some plans you can follow or introduce in your existing meal.

You can select a plan based on how much weight you want to reduce or your fitness goals.

- **5 & 1 Plan** - 5 fueling items and 1 serving of a protein-rich leafy meal.
- **4 & 2 & 1 Plan** - 4 fueling items, 2 lean protein and leafy meals, and 1 healthy snack.
- **5 & 2 & 1 Plan** - 5 fueling items, 2 lean protein meals, and 2 healthy snacks.
- **3 & 3 Plan** - 3 fueling items and 3 leafy green meals.

These plans are combinations of carefully picked fuelings, Lean and Green meals, and healthy snacks. Fueling in terms of food means consuming energizing meals/items that are carbohydrate controlled and low in fat. You may add one fruit or a low-fat dairy serving for a healthy snack.

These are structured to satisfy your appetite with fuelings, nourishing greens, and healthy snacks that do not make your meal boring. You may pick the right plan as per your fitness goals and health concerns.

Advantages of Lean and Green diet

These diet plans are most effective when it comes to losing weight quickly and keeping your weight in check. Apart from supporting your weight loss goal, it also improves the overall energy. Following this diet may help you in the following ways!

Prevents obesity and overweight risks
Obesity is unhealthy and brings a lot of risks like diabetes, asthma, heart disease, or stroke. Eating clean adds healthy items to your diet and prevents you from the health risks caused by obesity.

Helps in controlling blood pressure
Carbs and calories are among the two major causes of blood pressure. This meal plan mainly focuses on controlling the consumption of high carbs. Also, less intake of sodium and reduction in weight actively helps improve blood pressure.

Overall health improvement
The meal plans might be hard to follow in the initial stages, and you may experience fatigue due to a sudden change in diet. But over time, you will feel an overall improvement in your health. Along with weight loss, it reduces lethargy.

Nutrient consumption
Your body will be fueled with more nutrients with additional minerals and fiber. You will also get a boost in vitamins that come from these sources, as well as antioxidants. The primary benefit is the high amount of minerals, fiber, protein, antioxidants–without all the calories.

What can eat?

You may need to switch to healthier options under this diet.

Lean-green meals
As the name suggests, you can eat more beans and greens. Opting for non-starchy and low in-carb veggies like bean sprouts, cabbage, and eggplant. Besides, adding cauliflower, water chestnuts, broccoli, jicama, mushrooms, spinach, etc., is highly effective.

Lean meats
Lean meats are low in fat and should be a part of your new diet. Include lean beef, lamb, turkey, game meats, pork chop or tenderloin, chicken, ground meat in your meals.

Cooking oils
When preparing a diet meal, you also need to be picky with the cooking oil you use. To prepare your everyday meals, you can use avocado oil, olive oil, canola oil, or linseed oil.

Healthy fats
Olives, almonds, avocado, pistachios, reduced-fat margarine, and walnuts are excellent sources of healthy fats.

What not to eat

While it's essential to understand what to eat, you must know what not to eat as well. If you don't want to sabotage your progress, limit or cut the following items out of your diet.

Sugary Desserts
Reduce your sugar consumption. Maintain some distance from sweets like cookies, cakes, or ice cream. However, you can add yogurt and fresh fruits to your diet. They are the perfect alternatives to calm your sugar cravings.

High-calorie additions
Stay away from coconut oil, butter, or margarine as these are high in calories.

Alcohol
Any kind of alcohol consumption only adds to the calorie intake, so it is better to avoid drinking altogether.

Sweet beverages
Eliminate beverages like energy drinks, fruit juice, soda, sports drinks that have added sugar. Sweetened coffee or tea is also out of option.

Meal Plan 5 & 1

Week 1

Day-1	FUELING HACKS	Banana Cake Cashew Milk Almond Chocolate Bites Lemony Raspberry Compote Stuffed Eggs
	LEAN & GREEN MEAL	Lemony Chicken Fillets
Day-2	FUELING HACKS	Chocolate Fondue Crusted Bananas Basil Pesto Crackers Pumpkin Spiced Donuts Bread Dough in Amaretto
	LEAN & GREEN MEAL	Sautéed Lean Beef Steak with Onions
Day-3	FUELING HACKS	Creamy Kiwi Smoothie Orange Juice Soda Roasted Seeds Chocolate Peanut Butter Cups Watermelon Lemonade
	LEAN & GREEN MEAL	Lean Lamb Burgers
Day-4	FUELING HACKS	Cinnamon Bites Mini Lava Cakes Cherry Bread Pudding Mayo Onion and Cauliflower Dip Cherry Cream
	LEAN & GREEN MEAL	Beef Taco Meal
Day-5	FUELING HACKS	Cinnamon Banana Cake Apple Bread Tomato Avocado Salad Zucchini Taco Boats Creamy Caramel Cones
	LEAN & GREEN MEAL	Garlicky Lean Pork Ribs
Day-6	FUELING HACKS	Banana Bread Asian Noodle Salad Custard Filled Pears Minty Yogurt Vegan Marinara
	LEAN & GREEN MEAL	Rosemary Steak with Kale
Day-7	FUELING HACKS	Bread Cherry Pudding Cinnamon-flavored Wrapped Pears Rhubarb Delight Dark Chocolate Cherry Cookies Mayo Onion and Cauliflower Dip
	LEAN & GREEN MEAL	Roasted Cod with Capers

Week-2

Day-1	FUELING HACKS	Coconut Fat Bombs Creamy Cheesecake Tomato Avocado Salad Pumpkin Muffins Cherry Bread Pudding
	LEAN & GREEN MEAL	Chicken Greens Salad
Day-2	FUELING HACKS	Lime Poached Pears Pumpkin Spiced Donuts Minty Yogurt Rhubarb Delight Roasted Seeds
	LEAN & GREEN MEAL	Juicy Steak
Day-3	FUELING HACKS	Oat Milk Watermelon Lemonade Apple Bread Cherry Bread Pudding Coconut Fat Bombs
	LEAN & GREEN MEAL	Pork Burgers
Day-4	FUELING HACKS	Cinnamon-flavored Wrapped Pears Tomato Avocado Salad Mini Lava Cakes Lime Poached Pears Stuffed Eggs
	LEAN & GREEN MEAL	Thyme Shrimp
Day-5	FUELING HACKS	Almond Chocolate Bites Creamy Kiwi Smoothie Lemony Raspberry Compote Cherry Cream Basil Pesto Crackers
	LEAN & GREEN MEAL	Juicy Chicken Breast
Day-6	FUELING HACKS	Zucchini Taco Boats Creamy Cheesecake Banana Cake Chocolate Fondue Custard Filled Pears
	LEAN & GREEN MEAL	Turmeric Tuna Steaks
Day-7	FUELING HACKS	Bread Dough in Amaretto Chocolate Peanut Butter Cups Vegan Marinara Roasted Seeds Almond Chocolate Bites
	LEAN & GREEN MEAL	Shrimp with Snow Peas

Week-3

Day-1	**FUELING HACKS**	Coconut Fat Bombs Orange Juice Soda Watermelon Lemonade Bread Dough in Amaretto Chocolate Peanut Butter Cups
	LEAN & GREEN MEAL	Homemade Chicken Meatballs
Day-2	**FUELING HACKS**	Chocolate Fondue Custard Filled Pears Minty Yogurt Coconut Fat Bombs Pumpkin Muffins
	LEAN & GREEN MEAL	Chicken and Red Cabbage Stew
Day-3	**FUELING HACKS**	Pumpkin Spiced Donuts Basil Pesto Crackers Zucchini Taco Boats Cherry Cream Lime Poached Pears
	LEAN & GREEN MEAL	Lean Beef and Eggplant
Day-4	**FUELING HACKS**	Cashew Milk Zucchini Taco Boats Creamy Caramel Cones Basil Pesto Crackers Cherry Cream
	LEAN & GREEN MEAL	Chicken Cubes and Red Chard
Day-5	**FUELING HACKS**	Creamy Cheesecake Rhubarb Delight Banana Bread Dark Chocolate Cherry Cookies Roasted Seeds
	LEAN & GREEN MEAL	Italian Lean Beef Meatballs
Day-6	**FUELING HACKS**	Bread Dough in Amaretto Basil Pesto Crackers Cinnamon Bites Coconut Fat Bombs Cherry Bread Pudding
	LEAN & GREEN MEAL	Chicken Cubes and Red Chard
Day-7	**FUELING HACKS**	Cherry Cream Banana Cake Chocolate Fondue Cherry Bread Pudding Creamy Caramel Cones
	LEAN & GREEN MEAL	Tuna Casserole

Week-4

Day-1	**FUELING HACKS**	Creamy Kiwi Smoothie Bread Dough in Amaretto Zucchini Taco Boats Pumpkin Muffins Cherry Cream
	LEAN & GREEN MEAL	Lean Lamb Burgers
Day-2	**FUELING HACKS**	Chocolate Peanut Butter Cups Mini Lava Cakes Chocolate Fondue Custard Filled Pears Crusted Bananas
	LEAN & GREEN MEAL	Mango Tilapia Fillets
Day-3	**FUELING HACKS**	Cinnamon Banana Cake Stuffed Eggs Basil Pesto Crackers Creamy Kiwi Smoothie Roasted Seeds
	LEAN & GREEN MEAL	Garlicky Pork Tenderloin
Day-4	**FUELING HACKS**	Vegan Marinara Mayo Onion and Cauliflower Dip Lemony Raspberry Compote Mini Lava Cakes Cinnamon-flavored Wrapped Pears
	LEAN & GREEN MEAL	Beef Taco Meal
Day-5	**FUELING HACKS**	Rhubarb Delight Chocolate Fondue Dark Chocolate Cherry Cookies Bread Dough in Amaretto Apple Bread
	LEAN & GREEN MEAL	Lemon Cod Fillets
Day-6	**FUELING HACKS**	Creamy Cheesecake Vegan Marinara Pumpkin Spiced Donuts Lemony Raspberry Compote Asian Noodle Salad
	LEAN & GREEN MEAL	Garlicky Lean Pork Ribs
Day-7	**FUELING HACKS**	Cinnamon-flavored Wrapped Pears Pumpkin Muffins Basil Pesto Crackers Pumpkin Spiced Donuts Zucchini Taco Boats
	LEAN & GREEN MEAL	Pork Burgers

Meal Plan 4 & 2 & 1

Week 1

DAY 1	**FUELING HACKS**	Pumpkin Muffins Zucchini Taco Boats Cinnamon-flavored Wrapped Pears Mini Lava Cakes
	SNACK	2 Dill Pickles Spears
	LEAN & GREEN MEAL	Homemade Chicken Meatballs Sautéed Lean Beef Steak with Onions
DAY 2	**FUELING HACKS**	Creamy Kiwi Smoothie Vegan Marinara Cinnamon Banana Cake Cherry Cream
	SNACK	3 Celery Stalks
	LEAN & GREEN MEAL	Chicken Greens Salad Grilled Shrimp
DAY 3	**FUELING HACKS**	Zucchini Taco Boats Creamy Caramel Cones Rhubarb Delight Bread Cherry Pudding
	SNACK	½-ounce of Nuts
	LEAN & GREEN MEAL	Chicken Cubes and Red Chard Cheddar Broccoli Waffles
DAY 4	**FUELING HACKS**	Cinnamon Banana Cake Custard Filled Pears Stuffed Eggs Almond Chocolate Bites
	SNACK	Up to 3 Pieces of Sugar-Free Gum
	LEAN & GREEN MEAL	Shrimp Mix Garlicky Lean Pork Ribs
DAY 5	**FUELING HACKS**	Zucchini Taco Boats Mayo Onion and Cauliflower Dip Lemony Raspberry Compote Dark Chocolate Cherry Cookies
	SNACK	1 Fruit-Flavored Sugar-Free Popsicle
	LEAN & GREEN MEAL	Lemony Chicken Fillets Italian Sea Bass
DAY 6	**FUELING HACKS**	Cherry Bread Pudding Tomato Avocado Salad Cinnamon Bites Vegan Marinara
	SNACK	7 Walnut Halves
	LEAN & GREEN MEAL	Ground Beef Fry Baked Eggs with Spinach
DAY 7	**FUELING HACKS**	Asian Noodle Salad Bread Dough in Amaretto Minty Yogurt Cherry Cream
	SNACK	1 Cup Fresh, Cubed Melon
	LEAN & GREEN MEAL	Indian Spiced Cod Mustard Parmesan Turkey Breast

Week 2

DAY 1	**FUELING HACKS**	Rhubarb Delight Roasted Seeds Asian Noodle Salad Creamy Caramel Cones
	SNACK	Pistachios (20 Kernels)
	LEAN & GREEN MEAL	Lemony Chicken Fillets Limey Scallops
DAY 2	**FUELING HACKS**	Bread Dough in Amaretto Dark Chocolate Cherry Cookies Cinnamon Bites Oat Milk
	SNACK	1 Slice Whole-Meal Bread
	LEAN & GREEN MEAL	Pork Broccoli Fry Limey Trout Fillets
DAY 3	**FUELING HACKS**	Cherry Bread Pudding Cinnamon-flavored Wrapped Pears Chocolate Fondue Pumpkin Muffins
	SNACK	¾ Cup Cold Whole-Grain Cereal
	LEAN & GREEN MEAL	Garlicky Pork Tenderloin Zucchini Sushi Rolls
DAY 4	**FUELING HACKS**	Creamy Cheesecake Banana Cake Chocolate Fondue Cinnamon Bites
	SNACK	½ Cup Cooked Cereal
	LEAN & GREEN MEAL	Mustard Parmesan Turkey Breast Lettuce Seafood Wraps
DAY 5	**FUELING HACKS**	Almond Chocolate Bites Creamy Kiwi Smoothie Cashew Milk Basil Pesto Crackers
	SNACK	½ Cup Peas, Corn
	LEAN & GREEN MEAL	Chicken Greens Salad Sirloin Steak with Broccoli
DAY 6	**FUELING HACKS**	Creamy Kiwi Smoothie Orange Juice Soda Cinnamon Banana Cake Chocolate Peanut Butter Cups
	SNACK	1 cup winter squash
	LEAN & GREEN MEAL	Lean Beef and Eggplant Garlicky Lean Pork Ribs
DAY 7	**FUELING HACKS**	Almond Chocolate Bites Creamy Kiwi Smoothie Cinnamon-flavored Wrapped Pears Chocolate Fondue
	SNACK	¼ Large Baked Potato
	LEAN & GREEN MEAL	Chicken Wontons Thyme Shrimp

Week 3

DAY 1	**FUELING HACKS**	Crusted Bananas Apple Bread Dark Chocolate Cherry Cookies Oat Milk
	SNACK	⅓ Cup Cooked Brown Rice
	LEAN & GREEN MEAL	Fish Soup Sirloin Steak with Broccoli
DAY 2	**FUELING HACKS**	Creamy Kiwi Smoothie Creamy Caramel Cones Chocolate Peanut Butter Cups Banana Cake
	SNACK	⅓ Cup Cooked Whole-Wheat Pasta
	LEAN & GREEN MEAL	Lean Lamb Burgers Chicken and Red Cabbage Stew
DAY 3	**FUELING HACKS**	Coconut Fat Bombs Basil Pesto Crackers Cherry Bread Pudding Custard Filled Pears
	SNACK	½ Cup Cooked Beans Or Lentils
	LEAN & GREEN MEAL	Beef Taco Meal Tuna Casserole
DAY 4	**FUELING HACKS**	Cherry Cream Zucchini Taco Boats Cashew Milk Pumpkin Muffins
	SNACK	1 Small Piece Of Pear
	LEAN & GREEN MEAL	Juicy Steak Limey Scallops
DAY 5	**FUELING HACKS**	Asian Noodle Salad Pumpkin Spiced Donuts Coconut Fat Bombs Stuffed Eggs
	SNACK	1 Small Piece Of Apple
	LEAN & GREEN MEAL	Limey Trout Fillets Homemade Chicken Meatballs
DAY 6	**FUELING HACKS**	Vegan Marinara Rhubarb Delight Cherry Bread Pudding Cinnamon-flavored Wrapped Pears
	SNACK	¾ Cup Fresh Berries
	LEAN & GREEN MEAL	Chicken Greens Salad Limey Trout Fillets
DAY 7	**FUELING HACKS**	Creamy Cheesecake Banana Bread Crusted Bananas Minty Yogurt
	SNACK	½ Large Grapefruit
	LEAN & GREEN MEAL	Lean Beef and Eggplant Turmeric Tuna Steaks

Week 4

DAY 1	**FUELING HACKS**	Coconut Fat Bombs Basil Pesto Crackers Pumpkin Spiced Donuts Bread Dough in Amaretto
	SNACK	1 Small Piece of Orange
	LEAN & GREEN MEAL	Garlicky Pork Tenderloin Fish Soup
DAY 2	**FUELING HACKS**	Coconut Fat Bombs Basil Pesto Crackers Crusted Bananas Orange Juice Soda
	SNACK	½ Large Banana
	LEAN & GREEN MEAL	Chicken Cubes and Red Chard Mango Tilapia Fillets
DAY 3	**FUELING HACKS**	Minty Yogurt Rhubarb Delight Creamy Kiwi Smoothie Cinnamon Bites
	SNACK	2 Dill Pickles Spears
	LEAN & GREEN MEAL	Juicy Steak Lemon Cod Fillets
DAY 4	**FUELING HACKS**	Mayo Onion and Cauliflower Dip Lemony Raspberry Compote Custard Filled Pears Roasted Seeds
	SNACK	½-ounce Almonds
	LEAN & GREEN MEAL	Turmeric Tuna Steaks Pork Broccoli Fry
DAY 5	**FUELING HACKS**	Cherry Cream Banana Bread Cinnamon Banana Cake Coconut Fat Bombs
	SNACK	1 Small Banana
	LEAN & GREEN MEAL	Italian Lean Beef Meatballs Shrimp Mix
DAY 6	**FUELING HACKS**	Lime Poached Pears Vegan Marinara Pumpkin Muffins Cinnamon Bites
	SNACK	170g Low-Fat Yogurt
	LEAN & GREEN MEAL	Pork Burgers Shrimps Skewers
DAY 7	**FUELING HACKS**	Creamy Kiwi Smoothie Creamy Cheesecake Vegan Marinara Dark Chocolate Cherry Cookies
	SNACK	½ Cup Fat-Free Evaporated Milk
	LEAN & GREEN MEAL	Ground Beef Fry Simple Oregano Chicken Strips

Chapter 1 Breakfast Recipes

Egg Broccoli Bread

Prep Time: 15 minutes | **Cook Time:** 50 minutes | **Servings**: 3

Ingredients:
¼ cup shredded reduced-fat cheddar
3 cups small broccoli florets
1 teaspoons cayenne pepper
4 eggs
1 teaspoon black pepper
½ cup unsweetened almond milk
Salt, to taste

Directions:
Preheat your oven to 375 degrees F. Grease the baking dish with oil or cooking spray.
Add 2 tablespoons of water and broccoli florets in a microwave-safe bowl and microwave them for about 4 minutes.
When done, strain the broccoli florets and then arrange to the greased baking dish; sprinkle cheese over them.
In a large bowl, beat the eggs with the black pepper, cayenne pepper, salt and almond milk; pour the egg mixture over the broccoli florets.
Bake the food in the oven for about 45 minutes.
Slice before serving.

Per serving: Calories: 146; Carbs: 6.66 g; Protein: 11.65 g; Total Fat: 8.34 g; Fiber: 1.6 g; Sugar: 3.96 g; Sodium: 236 mg; Potassium: 220 mg; Calcium (Ca): 228 mg; Vitamin B-12: 1.16 µg; Vitamin D: 66 IU

Blueberry Pancakes

Prep Time: 10 minutes | **Cook Time:** 10 minutes | **Servings**: 3

Ingredients:
2 tablespoons grape seed oil
1 cup coconut milk
½ cup blueberries
½ cup alkaline water
½ cup agave
2 cups spelled flour
¼ teaspoons sea moss

Directions:
In a bowl, mix up the spelled flour, agave, grape seed oil and sea moss.
Add the milk and alkaline water to the agave mixture until you get the consistent mixture you like.
Crimp the blueberries into the batter.
In the skillet over medium heat, lightly coat it with the grape seed oil.
Pour the batter into this skillet, and then let them cook for approximately 5 minutes on each side.
Serve and enjoy.

Per serving: Calories: 344; Carbs: 63.67 g; Protein: 10.31 g; Total Fat: 5.06 g; Fiber: 6.4 g; Sugar: 6.72 g; Sodium: 39 mg; Potassium: 264 mg; Calcium (Ca): 328 mg; Vitamin B-12: 0.27 µg; Vitamin D: 1 IU

Oat Breads with Bananas

Prep Time: 10 minutes | **Cook Time:** 0 | **Servings**: 3

Ingredients:
2 ripe medium-sized bananas
1 cup roasted cashews
A dash of cinnamon
2 teaspoons flax meals
4 pieces' oat bread
2 teaspoons pure honey
Salt

Directions:
Peel the bananas and then cut them into slices.
Toast the oat bread pieces.
In a food processor, add the salt and cashews, puree them until they are smooth.
Spread cashews mixture on the toasted bread, arrange the banana slices on them and top them with the flax meals and a dash of cinnamon evenly.
Serve the breads with honey.

Per serving: Calories: 467; Carbs: 56.68 g; Protein: 12.51 g; Total Fat: 24.04 g; Fiber: 5.2 g; Sugar: 18.06 g; Sodium: 258 mg; Potassium: 624 mg; Calcium (Ca): 85 mg; Vitamin B-12: 0 µg; Vitamin D: 0 IU

Bacon and Brussels Sprout Meal

Prep Time: 10 minutes | **Cook Time:** 15 minutes | **Servings**: 3

Ingredients:
1½ tablespoons apple cider vinegar
Salt
2 minced shallots
2 minced garlic cloves
3 medium eggs
12-ounce sliced Brussels sprouts
Black pepper
2-ounce chopped bacon
1 tablespoon melted butter

Directions:
In the skillet, heat the bacon over medium heat until crispy, then transfer them to a suitable plate.
Still in the skillet, sauté the garlic and shallots for almost 30 seconds.
Stir in apple cider vinegar, Brussels sprouts, salt, black pepper and cook for about 5 minutes.
Add the bacon back and cook for 5 minutes longer; then stir in the butter and set a hole at the center.
Crash the eggs to the pan and let cook fully.
Enjoy!

Per serving: Calories: 212; Carbs: 13.56 g; Protein: 11.61 g; Total Fat: 13.97 g; Fiber: 4.9 g; Sugar: 3.59 g; Sodium: 421 mg; Potassium: 558 mg; Calcium (Ca): 83 mg; Vitamin B-12: 0.4 µg; Vitamin D: 39 IU

Pumpkin Waffles

Prep Time: 15 minutes | **Cook Time:** 5 minutes | **Servings**: 4

Ingredients:
2 medium bananas
1½ teaspoons ground cinnamon
½ cup coconut flour
2 tablespoons olive oil
½ teaspoon ground cloves
¾ teaspoon ground ginger
1 teaspoon baking soda
½ teaspoon ground nutmeg
½ cup almond flour
5 large eggs
¾ cup almond milk
½ cup pumpkin puree
Salt

Directions:
Peel and slice the bananas.
Preheat the waffle iron and then grease it with the oil.
In a large bowl, mix up the coconut flour, almond flour, baking soda, cinnamon, ground cloves, ground ginger and ground nutmeg.
In a blender, put the remaining ingredients and pulse till smooth; add the flour mixture and pulse until smooth.
In preheated waffle iron, add the required quantity of mixture. Cook the food for 4 to 5 minutes.
Cook the remaining mixture with the same steps.
Serve and enjoy.

Per serving: Calories: 321; Carbs: 22.75 g; Protein: 13.53 g; Total Fat: 20.95 g; Fiber: 3.7 g; Sugar: 12.41 g; Sodium: 544 mg; Potassium: 535 mg; Calcium (Ca): 149 mg; Vitamin B-12: 1.12 µg; Vitamin D: 70 IU

Strawberry Yogurt Meal

Prep Time: 10 minutes | **Cook Time:** 0 | **Servings**: 4

Ingredients:
4 cups fat-free plain Greek yogurt
1 cup strawberries
8 tablespoons flax meal
4 tablespoons honey
8 tablespoons walnuts

Directions:
Chop the walnuts. Wash and slice the strawberries.
Distribute 2 cups of the yogurt into the serving bowls.
Neatly layer the flax meal and the walnut in the middle.
Add a drizzle of ½ of the honey before covering it with the last layer of yogurt.
Add the remaining honey on top of the yogurt to add color when you serve.

Per serving: Calories: 346; Carbs: 41.72 g; Protein: 17.61 g; Total Fat: 13.77 g; Fiber: 1.8 g; Sugar: 36.43 g; Sodium: 184 mg; Potassium: 752 mg; Calcium (Ca): 487 mg; Vitamin B-12: 1.48 µg; Vitamin D: 2 IU

Spinach Waffles

Prep Time: 10 minutes | **Cook Time:** 20 minutes | **Servings**: 4

Ingredients:
4 oz. frozen spinach
½ cup part-skim Mozzarella cheese
1 large egg
1 cup ricotta cheese
¼ cup low-fat grated Parmesan cheese
1 garlic clove
Salt
Pepper

Directions:
Crumble the ricotta cheese and shred the mozzarella cheese.
Mince the garlic.
Preheat a mini waffle iron and then grease it.
In a suitable bowl, add all the ingredients and beat until well mixed.
Place ¼ of the prepared mixture into preheated waffle iron and cook for about 4 to 5 minutes, or until golden brown.
Cook the remaining mixture with the same steps.
Serve warm.

Per serving: Calories: 140; Carbs: 5.24 g; Protein: 17.68 g; Total Fat: 5.61 g; Fiber: 1.5 g; Sugar: 1.37 g; Sodium: 383 mg; Potassium: 232 mg; Calcium (Ca): 461 mg; Vitamin B-12: 0.53 µg; Vitamin D: 13 IU

Eggs Avocado Toast

Prep Time: 15 minutes | **Cook Time:** 5 minutes | **Servings**: 4

Ingredients:
4 whole-wheat bread slices
4 hard-boiled eggs
¼ teaspoons lemon juice
1 avocado
Salt
Ground black pepper

Directions:
Cut the avocado in half and scoop out the flesh.
Peel the eggs and cut them into slices.
In a bowl, add the avocado flesh and mash the flesh with a fork.
In another bowl, mix up the lemon juice, pepper and salt.
In a nonstick fry pan over medium-high heat, toast the bread slices for 2 minutes on each side.
When toasted, spread the avocado mixture over each slice evenly and top each bread slice with egg slices.
Serve and enjoy.

Per serving: Calories: 250; Carbs: 21.85 g; Protein: 10.07 g; Total Fat: 14.46 g; Fiber: 5.4 g; Sugar: 2.17 g; Sodium: 218 mg; Potassium: 411 mg; Calcium (Ca): 42 mg; Vitamin B-12: 0.56 µg; Vitamin D: 44 IU

Spinach Egg Bread

Prep Time: 5 minutes | **Cook Time:** 10 minutes | **Servings**: 4

Ingredients:
20 pieces' Swiss chard leaves
4 pieces of rice bread
20 pieces' spinach leaves
4 tablespoons parsley
4 egg whites
1 teaspoons olive oil
Salt
Pepper
Dried mint

Directions:
In a pan, boil 2 cups of water.
Carefully crack an egg into a small bowl.
Lower the bowl towards the heated water, and gently pour the egg into the water.
Do the same with the other eggs.
Poach the eggs for almost 4 minutes.
After that, gently take one egg at a time and transfer them to a suitable plate.
Do the same with the remaining eggs.
Toast the bread.
Chop the parsley and then sauté the leaves in a suitable pan for almost 6 minutes.
When done, make a layer of the sautéed greens and chopped parsley on top of the toasted bread.
Put the poached eggs above the bed of greens. Sprinkle each serving with ground pepper, sea salt, and dried mint.

Per serving: Calories: 86; Carbs: 11.29 g; Protein: 9.46 g; Total Fat: 1.89 g; Fiber: 5.1 g; Sugar: 3.12 g; Sodium: 646 mg; Potassium: 1264 mg; Calcium (Ca): 180 mg; Vitamin B-12: 0.03 µg; Vitamin D: 0 IU

Granola with Persimmon

Prep Time: 5 minutes | **Cook Time:** 5 minutes | **Servings**: 4

Ingredients:
4 oz. Greek-style yogurt
4 tablespoons oatmeal
60g fresh persimmons
30ml water

Directions:
Put the oatmeal in the pan without any fat.
Toast them, stirring constantly, until golden brown.
Transfer them to a suitable plate and let them cool down briefly.
In a bowl with water, put the peeled persimmons and mix the whole thing into a fine puree.
Add the yogurt, toasted oatmeal, and then puree in layers in a bowl. Enjoy.

Per serving: Calories: 121; Carbs: 22.83 g; Protein: 5.57 g; Total Fat: 1.33 g; Fiber: 2.6 g; Sugar: 8.29 g; Sodium: 143 mg; Potassium: 192 mg; Calcium (Ca): 50 mg; Vitamin B-12: 0.12 µg; Vitamin D: 0 IU

Coffee Banana Bread

Prep Time: 15 minutes | **Cook Time:** 40 minutes | **Servings**: 6

Ingredients:
2 ripe bananas, mashed
1 cup brewed coffee
1 tablespoons chia seeds
6 tablespoons water
½ cup vegan butter
½ cup maple syrup
1 ¾ cups flour
2 teaspoons baking powder
1 teaspoons cinnamon powder
1 teaspoons allspice
½ teaspoons salt

Directions:
Preheat the oven to 350 degrees F. Line the baking pan with parchment paper.
In a bowl, add the chia seeds and 6 tablespoons of water, stir well and soak them.
In a mixing bowl, mix the vegan butter and maple syrup until the mixture turns fluffy; mix in the chia seeds and mashed bananas, then add the Coffee.
Sift the flour, baking powder, cinnamon powder, allspice, and salt, and then gradually add them into the bowl with the wet ingredients.
Mix the ingredients well, and then pour over the baking pan lined with parchment paper.
Bake the food for 30 to 40 minutes or until the toothpick comes out clean after inserting in the bread.
Allow the bread to cool before serving.

Per serving: Calories: 376; Carbs: 55.85 g; Protein: 4.48 g; Total Fat: 15.94 g; Fiber: 2.4 g; Sugar: 20.8 g; Sodium: 203 mg; Potassium: 434 mg; Calcium (Ca): 121 mg; Vitamin B-12: 0.03 µg; Vitamin D: 11 IU

Chicken Avocado Salad

Prep Time: 15 minutes | **Cook Time:** 0 | **Servings**: 4

Ingredients:
10 oz. diced cooked chicken
½ cup plain Greek yogurt
3 oz. chopped avocado
12 teaspoons garlic powder
¼ teaspoons salt
1 teaspoons pepper
1 tablespoon + 1 teaspoons lime juice
¼ cup fresh cilantro, chopped

Directions:
In a bowl, mix all ingredients. Refrigerate the mixture until ready to serve.
Apportion the chicken salad and serve with your favorite greens.

Per serving: Calories: 245; Carbs: 9.69 g; Protein: 22.86 g; Total Fat: 12.91 g; Fiber: 2.5 g; Sugar: 0.86 g; Sodium: 216 mg; Potassium: 409 mg; Calcium (Ca): 40 mg; Vitamin B-12: 0.32 µg; Vitamin D: 1 IU

Breakfast Donuts

Prep Time: 5 minutes | **Cook Time:** 5 minutes | **Serves:** 4

Ingredients:
43 g cream cheese
2 eggs
2 tablespoons almond flour
2 tablespoons erythritol
1 ½ tablespoons coconut flour
½ teaspoon baking powder
½ teaspoon vanilla extract
5 drops swerve (liquid form)
2 strips bacon, fried until crispy

Directions:
Rub canola oil over the donut maker and turn it on. Pulse all ingredients except bacon in a blender or food processor until smooth (it should take around 1 minute).
Pour batter into donut maker, leaving 1/10 in each round for rising. Leave for 3 minutes before flipping each donut.
Leave for another 2 minutes or until the fork comes out clean when piercing them. Take donuts out and let cool. Crumble bacon into bits and use it to top donuts.

Per serving: Calories: 129; Carbs: 6.37 g; Protein: 5.69 g; Total Fat: 8.96 g; Fiber: 0.2 g; Sugar: 5.28 g; Sodium: 141 mg; Potassium: 177 mg; Calcium (Ca): 61 mg; Vitamin B-12: 1.93 µg; Vitamin D: 26 IU

Cheesy Bacon Meal

Prep Time: 10 minutes | **Cook Time:** 22 minutes | **Serves:** 12

Ingredients:
6 strips bacon, pan-fried until cooked but still malleable
4 eggs
60g cheddar cheese
40g cream cheese, grated
2 jalapenos, sliced and seeds removed
2 tablespoons canola oil
¼ teaspoon onion powder
¼ teaspoon garlic powder
Dash of salt and pepper

Directions:
Preheat oven to 375ºF.
In a suitable bowl, beat together eggs, cream cheese, jalapenos (minus 6 slices), canola oil, onion powder, garlic powder, and salt and pepper.
Use the leftover bacon to grease on a muffin tray, rubbing it into each insert. Place bacon-wrapped inside the parameters of each insert.
Pour the beaten mixture halfway up each bacon bowl. Garnish each bacon bowl with Parmesan cheese and leftover jalapeno slices (placing one on top of each).
Leave in the oven for about 22 minutes, or until the egg is thoroughly cooked and cheese is bubbly. Remove from oven and let cool until edible. Enjoy!

Per serving: Calories: 74; Carbs: 2.35 g; Protein: 3.23 g; Total Fat: 5.93 g; Fiber: 0.6 g; Sugar: 1.41 g; Sodium: 142 mg; Potassium: 89 mg; Calcium (Ca): 42 mg; Vitamin B-12: 0.2 µg; Vitamin D: 13 IU

Zucchini Walnut Muffins

Prep Time: 10 minutes | **Cook Time:** 25 minutes | **Serves:** 16

Ingredients:
1 tablespoon ground flaxseed
3 tablespoons water
¼ cup walnut butter
3 medium over-ripe bananas
2 small grated zucchinis
½ cup almond milk
1 teaspoon vanilla extract
2 cups coconut flour
1 tablespoon baking powder
1 teaspoon cinnamon
¼ teaspoon sea salt

Directions:
Tune the temperature of your oven to 375ºF. Grease the suitable muffin tray with the cooking oil.
In a suitable bowl, mix the flaxseed with water.
In another glass bowl, mash the bananas, then stir in the remaining ingredients.
Properly mix and then divide the mixture into the muffin tray. Bake it for 25 minutes.
Serve fresh.

Per serving: Calories: 60; Carbs: 7.7 g; Protein: 0.7 g; Total Fat: 3.39 g; Fiber: 1.2 g; Sugar: 4.19 g; Sodium: 97 mg; Potassium: 268 mg; Calcium (Ca): 68 mg; Vitamin B-12: 0.1 µg; Vitamin D: 5 IU

Millet Coconut Porridge

Prep Time: 10 minutes | **Cook Time:** 20 minutes | **Serves:** 2

Ingredients:
Sea salt
1 tablespoon chopped coconuts
½ cup almond milk
½ cup rinsed and drained millet
1-½ cups water
3 drops liquid swerve

Directions:
Sauté the millet in a non-stick skillet for about 3 minutes. Add salt and water, then stir. Let the meal boil, then reduce the amount of heat.
Cook for almost 15 minutes, then add the remaining ingredients. Stir—Cook the meal for 4 extra minutes. Serve the meal with a topping of the chopped nuts.

Per serving: Calories: 87; Carbs: 17.34 g; Protein: 1.96 g; Total Fat: 1.2 g; Fiber: 0.9 g; Sugar: 6.64 g; Sodium: 131 mg; Potassium: 91 mg; Calcium (Ca): 125 mg; Vitamin B-12: 0.75 µg; Vitamin D: 25 IU

Pumpkin Banana Quinoa

Prep Time: 10 minutes | **Cook Time:** 0 minutes | **Serves:** 2

Ingredients:
1 cup cooked quinoa
1 cup almond milk
1 large mashed banana
¼ cup pumpkin puree
1 teaspoon pumpkin spice
2 teaspoons chia seeds

Directions:
In a container, mix all the ingredients. Seal the lid, then shake the container properly to mix. Refrigerate overnight. Serve.

Per serving: Calories: 338; Carbs: 44.25 g; Protein: 13.27 g; Total Fat: 13.64 g; Fiber: 5.8 g; Sugar: 15.54 g; Sodium: 98 mg; Potassium: 690 mg; Calcium (Ca): 177 mg; Vitamin B-12: 0.55 µg; Vitamin D: 2 IU

Squash Hash

Prep Time: 2 minutes | **Cook Time:** 10 minutes | **Serves:** 2

Ingredients:
1 teaspoon onion powder
½ cup chopped onion
2 cups spaghetti squash
½ teaspoon sea salt

Directions:
Using paper towels, squeeze extra moisture from spaghetti squash. Place the squash into a suitable bowl, then add the salt, onion, and onion powder.
Stir properly to mix them. Spray a non-stick cooking skillet with cooking spray, then place it over moderate heat. Add the spaghetti squash to the pan.
Cook the squash for about 5 minutes. Flip the hash browns using a spatula. Cook for almost 5 minutes until the desired crispness is reached. Serve.

Per serving: Calories: 47; Carbs: 10.61 g; Protein: 1.09 g; Total Fat: 0.62 g; Fiber: 2.2 g; Sugar: 4.09 g; Sodium: 601 mg; Potassium: 163 mg; Calcium (Ca): 35 mg; Vitamin B-12: 0 µg; Vitamin D: 0 IU

Mango Oatmeal

Prep Time: 5 minutes | **Cook Time:** 5 minutes | **Serves:** 2

Ingredients:
1½ cups water
½ cup 5-minute steel cut oats
¼ cup almond milk
1 tablespoon pure maple syrup
1 teaspoon sesame seeds
Dash ground cinnamon
1 mango, stripped, pitted, and divide into slices
1 tablespoon unsweetened coconut flakes

Directions:
In a frying pan over high heat, boil water. Put the oats and lower the heat. Cook, occasionally stirring, for 5 minutes.
Put in the almond milk, maple syrup, and salt to combine. Get two bowls and sprinkle with the sesame seeds and cinnamon. Top with sliced mango and coconut flakes.

Per serving: Calories: 222; Carbs: 52.3 g; Protein: 6.02 g; Total Fat: 4.25 g; Fiber: 7.2 g; Sugar: 32.96 g; Sodium: 37 mg; Potassium: 476 mg; Calcium (Ca): 124 mg; Vitamin B-12: 0.38 µg; Vitamin D: 13 IU

Ricotta Egg Cups

Prep Time: 10 minutes | **Cook Time:** 1 hour | **Serves:** 6

Ingredients:
6 eggs, whisked
1½ lbs. ricotta cheese, soft
½ pound swerve
1 teaspoon vanilla extract
½ teaspoon baking powder
Cooking spray

Directions:
In a suitable bowl, mix the eggs, ricotta, and the other ingredients except for the cooking spray and whisk well.
Grease 4 ramekins with the cooking spray, pour the ricotta cream in each and bake at 360ºF for 1 hour. Serve cold.

Per serving: Calories: 359; Carbs: 34.11 g; Protein: 18.4 g; Total Fat: 16.2 g; Fiber: 0.1 g; Sugar: 26.3 g; Sodium: 169 mg; Potassium: 236 mg; Calcium (Ca): 315 mg; Vitamin B-12: 0.75 µg; Vitamin D: 45 IU

Quinoa Blueberry Porridge

Prep Time: 5 minutes | **Cook Time:** 25 minutes | **Serves:** 2

Ingredients:
2 cups of almond milk
1 cup rinsed quinoa
⅛ teaspoon ground cinnamon
1 cup fresh blueberries

Directions:
In a suitable saucepan, boil the almond milk over high heat. Add the quinoa to the milk, then bring the mixture to a boil.
You then let it simmer for 15 minutes on medium heat until the milk is reducing. Add the cinnamon, then mix it properly in the saucepan.
Cover the saucepan and cook for almost 8 minutes until the milk is completely absorbed. Add in the blueberries, then cook for almost 30 more seconds. Serve.

Per serving: Calories: 439; Carbs: 77.53 g; Protein: 20.81 g; Total Fat: 5.6 g; Fiber: 7.8 g; Sugar: 19.84 g; Sodium: 108 mg; Potassium: 918 mg; Calcium (Ca): 345 mg; Vitamin B-12: 1.23 µg; Vitamin D: 115 IU

Barley Coconut Porridge

Prep Time: 15 minutes | **Cook Time:** 5 minutes | **Serves:** 2

Ingredients:
1 cup almond milk
1 small peeled and sliced banana
½ cup barley
3 drops liquid swerve
¼ cup chopped coconuts

Directions:
In a suitable bowl, properly mix barley with half of the almond milk and swerve. Cover the mixing bowl, then refrigerate for about 6 hours.
In a suitable saucepan, mix the barley mixture with almond milk—Cook for almost about 5 minutes on moderate heat. Then top it with the chopped coconuts and the banana slices. Serve.

Per serving: Calories: 305; Carbs: 58.48 g; Protein: 9.56 g; Total Fat: 4.8 g; Fiber: 9.4 g; Sugar: 14.66 g; Sodium: 89 mg; Potassium: 557 mg; Calcium (Ca): 162 mg; Vitamin B-12: 0.55 µg; Vitamin D: 2 IU

Chapter 2 Poultry Recipes

Chicken and Red Cabbage Stew

Prep Time: 10 minutes | **Cook Time:** 40 minutes | **Servings**: 4

Ingredients:
1 cup red cabbage, chopped
10 oz. chicken thighs, boneless, chopped
3 spring onions, chopped
1 teaspoons salt
1 teaspoons chili powder
½ cup of water
1 tablespoon olive oil
1 teaspoons ground black pepper

Directions:
In the saucepan, heat the olive oil; add the chicken thighs, season them salt and pepper, then cook the thighs for 3 minutes on each side.
Add the resting ingredients, mix well, cover the pan and then reduce the heat to low.
Cook the mix for about 34 minutes.
When done, serve and enjoy.

Per serving: Calories: 200; Carbs: 3.35 g; Protein: 12.38 g; Total Fat: 15.32 g; Fiber: 1.1 g; Sugar: 1.17 g; Sodium: 667 mg; Potassium: 251 mg; Calcium (Ca): 31 mg; Vitamin B-12: 0.44 µg; Vitamin D: 2 IU

Lemon Chicken Thighs

Prep Time: 10 minutes | **Cook Time:** 55 minutes | **Servings**: 4

Ingredients:
3 spring onions, chopped
4 chicken thighs, skinless, boneless
1 teaspoon lemongrass, ground
1 teaspoon lemon zest, grated
1 tablespoon lemon juice
½ teaspoons salt
½ teaspoons ground black pepper
1 teaspoon olive oil
1 teaspoon ground paprika
1 teaspoon minced garlic
¼ cup of water

Directions:
In a roasting pan, mix the chicken thighs with other recipe ingredients.
Set the oven at 365 degrees F; bake the food in the oven for 55 minutes.
Divide between plates and serve.

Per serving: Calories: 349; Carbs: 2.66 g; Protein: 25.09 g; Total Fat: 26 g; Fiber: 0.6 g; Sugar: 0.75 g; Sodium: 415 mg; Potassium: 375 mg; Calcium (Ca): 25 mg; Vitamin B-12: 0.92 µg; Vitamin D: 4 IU

Jerk Chicken Drumettes

Prep Time: 20 minutes | **Cook Time:** 50 minutes | **Serves:** 10

Ingredients:
10 chicken legs
½ teaspoon ground nutmeg
½ teaspoon ground cinnamon
1 teaspoon ground allspice
1 teaspoon black pepper
1 tablespoon fresh thyme
1½ tablespoons brown swerve
¼ cup soy sauce
⅓ cup fresh lime juice
1 tablespoon ginger, sliced
2 habanera peppers, remove the stem
4 garlic cloves, peeled and smashed
6 green onions, chopped

Directions:
Add chicken into the large zip-lock bag.
Add remaining ingredients for seasoning into the food processor and process.
Pour mixture over chicken. Seal this bag and shake well to coat the chicken and place it in the refrigerator overnight.
Set the oven's temperature 375 degrees F, timer for 50 minutes. Press start to preheat the oven.
Line baking sheet with foil. Arrange marinated chicken legs on a baking sheet and bake for 45-50 minutes.
Serve and enjoy.

Per serving: Calories: 365; Carbs: 7.93 g; Protein: 52.15 g; Total Fat: 12.69 g; Fiber: 1.4 g; Sugar: 3.53 g; Sodium: 359 mg; Potassium: 775 mg; Calcium (Ca): 61 mg; Vitamin B-12: 1.51 µg; Vitamin D: 3 IU

Chicken Cubes and Red Chard

Prep Time: 15 minutes | **Cook Time:** 20 minutes | **Servings**: 4

Ingredients:
1-pound chicken breast, skinless, boneless, and cubed
1 cup red chard, torn
1 tablespoon avocado oil
1 teaspoon sweet paprika
1 tablespoons lemon juice
¼ teaspoons salt

Directions:
In the pan, heat with the oil over medium heat; add the chicken cubes and cook them for 10 minutes.
Add other recipe ingredients and sauté them for 10 minutes longer.
Serve.

Per serving: Calories: 159; Carbs: 0.91 g; Protein: 25.43 g; Total Fat: 5.45 g; Fiber: 0.4 g; Sugar: 0.25 g; Sodium: 223 mg; Potassium: 337 mg; Calcium (Ca): 19 mg; Vitamin B-12: 0.44 µg; Vitamin D: 12 IU

Chicken Wontons

Prep Time: 25 minutes | **Cook Time:** 12 minutes | **Serves:** 4

Ingredients:
1 cup all-purpose flour
¼ lb. boneless skinless chicken breast
1 egg
1 green onion
1 tablespoon French beans
1 tablespoon carrots
½ teaspoon pepper powder
¼ teaspoon soy sauce
½ teaspoon cornstarch
1 teaspoon sesame seed oil

Directions:
Dice all of your vegetables, beans, and chicken into the smallest pieces possible.
Mix flour, salt, and a little hot water to create a stiff dough. Cover and set aside.
Beat the egg in a suitable bowl. Add all other ingredients, except for the sesame seed oil, to the egg bowl and mix well.
Add the sesame seed oil to the mix and mix again.
Roll your dough flat and use a cookie cutter to cut it into circles about 6 inches in diameter. You can also use pre-made wonton wrappers.
At 360 degrees F, preheat your air fryer. Scoop a little mixture into the center of each circle.
Use your fingers to wet the edges of the circles. Fold them over the stuffing and press to close.
Cook in the air fryer for 12 minutes, flipping them after 7 minutes.

Per serving: Calories: 188; Carbs: 28.25 g; Protein: 11.95 g; Total Fat: 2.68 g; Fiber: 2.2 g; Sugar: 1.22 g; Sodium: 46 mg; Potassium: 253 mg; Calcium (Ca): 24 mg; Vitamin B-12: 0.16 µg; Vitamin D: 9 IU

Turmeric Chicken Fillets

Prep Time: 10 minutes | **Cook Time:** 20 minutes | **Servings**: 2

Ingredients:
1 tablespoons almonds, chopped
1 teaspoons turmeric powder
¼ cup organic almond milk
½ teaspoons salt
1 tablespoons olive oil
½ teaspoons white pepper
6 oz. chicken fillet, sliced

Directions:
In the pan, heat the oil over medium heat; add the chicken slices and cook them for 5 minutes on each side.
Add other ingredients and cook them for 10 minutes longer.
Serve and enjoy.

Per serving: Calories: 206; Carbs: 4.4 g; Protein: 15.36 g; Total Fat: 14.38 g; Fiber: 0.7 g; Sugar: 2.7 g; Sodium: 654 mg; Potassium: 503 mg; Calcium (Ca): 68 mg; Vitamin B-12: 0.85 µg; Vitamin D: 22 IU

Chicken Mushroom Kabobs

Prep Time: 15 minutes | **Cook Time:** 20 minutes | **Serves:** 4

Ingredients:
2 chicken breasts, cut into cubes
⅓ cup honey
⅓ cup soy sauce
Sesame seeds
6 mushrooms
1 each- red, yellow, and green bell pepper
Cooking spray
Salt to taste

Directions:
Spray the chicken cubes with cooking spray and season with salt
Transfer to a suitable bowl and mix chicken with honey, soy sauce, and sesame seeds. Cut mushrooms in half.
Preheat your air fryer to 340 degrees F.
Add chicken, peppers, and mushrooms onto the skewers, alternating each one until the skewers are full.
Cook in the hot air fryer for 20 minutes, turning the kabobs at the halfway mark.

Per serving: Calories: 330; Carbs: 32.286 g; Protein: 33.74 g; Total Fat: 7.68 g; Fiber: 1.3 g; Sugar: 29.28 g; Sodium: 423 mg; Potassium: 726 mg; Calcium (Ca): 21 mg; Vitamin B-12: 0.3 µg; Vitamin D: 3 IU

Juicy Chicken Breast

Prep Time: 15 minutes | **Cook Time:** 25 minutes | **Serves:** 8

Ingredients:
4 chicken breasts, boneless
1 tablespoon olive oil
For Rub:
1 teaspoon garlic powder
1 teaspoon onion powder
4 teaspoons brown swerve
4 teaspoons paprika
1 teaspoon black pepper
1 teaspoon salt

Directions:
Set the oven's temperature at 390 degrees F, timer for 30 minutes. Press start to preheat the oven.
Brush chicken breasts with olive oil. In a small bowl, whisk together rub ingredients and rub all over chicken breasts.
Arrange chicken breasts on a roasting pan and bake for 12-15 minutes or until internal temperature reaches 165 degrees F.
Serve and enjoy.

Per serving: Calories: 278; Carbs: 2.86 g; Protein: 30.68 g; Total Fat: 15.32 g; Fiber: 0.6 g; Sugar: 0.17 g; Sodium: 384 mg; Potassium: 362 mg; Calcium (Ca): 22 mg; Vitamin B-12: 0.49 µg; Vitamin D: 23 IU

Balsamic Chicken

Prep Time: 12 minutes | **Cook Time:** 25 minutes | **Serves:** 4

Ingredients:
4 chicken breasts, skinless and boneless
2 teaspoons dried oregano
2 garlic cloves, minced
½ cup balsamic vinegar
2 tablespoons soy sauce
¼ cup oil
Black pepper
Salt

Directions:
Set the oven's temperature 390 degrees F, timer for 25 minutes. Press start to preheat the oven.
In a suitable bowl, mix together soy sauce, salt, oil, black pepper, oregano, garlic, and vinegar. Place chicken in a baking dish and pour soy sauce mixture over chicken. Let it sit for 10 minutes. Bake chicken for 25 minutes. Serve and enjoy.

Per serving: Calories: 500; Carbs: 8.62 g; Protein: 62.12 g; Total Fat: 22.24 g; Fiber: 0.6 g; Sugar: 6.34 g; Sodium: 251 mg; Potassium: 985 mg; Calcium (Ca): 37 mg; Vitamin B-12: 0.57 µg; Vitamin D: 3 IU

Buffalo Chicken Meatballs

Prep Time: 10 minutes | **Cook Time:** 10 minutes | **Serves:** 4

Ingredients:
1-pound ground chicken
4 garlic cloves
1 package ranch seasoning
1 cup seasoned breadcrumbs
1 cup hot sauce
1 cup fat-free ranch dressing
½ cup blue cheese crumbles

Directions:
Mince the garlic.
Combine garlic, ranch seasoning, and breadcrumbs in a suitable bowl.
Add the chicken and knead the ingredients together.
Roll into small balls.
Cook for almost 360 degrees F for 5 minutes using the air fryer.
Toss the prepared meatballs in the hot sauce and cook up to another 5 minutes.
Mix together ranch dressing and blue cheese crumbles.
Drizzle ranch mix over meatballs before serving.

Per serving: Calories: 356; Carbs: 37.52 g; Protein: 32.05 g; Total Fat: 8.13 g; Fiber: 1.5 g; Sugar: 5.63 g; Sodium: 993 mg; Potassium: 467 mg; Calcium (Ca): 186 mg; Vitamin B-12: 0.79 µg; Vitamin D: 29 IU

Crackling Chicken Breast

Prep Time: 15 minutes | **Cook Time:** 35 minutes | **Serves:** 4

Ingredients:
4 chicken breasts, skinless and boneless
½ cup butter, cut into pieces
1 cup cracker crumbs
3 eggs, lightly beaten
Pepper
Salt

Directions:
Set the oven's temperature 375 degrees F, timer for 35 minutes. Press start to preheat the oven.
Add cracker crumbs and eggs in 2 separate shallow dishes.
Mix cracker crumbs with salt and pepper.
Dip chicken in the eggs and then coat with cracker crumb.
Arrange coated chicken into the 9*13-inch baking dish.
Spread butter pieces on top of the chicken and bake for 30-35 minutes.
Serve and enjoy.

Per serving: Calories: 581; Carbs: 0.76 g; Protein: 65.64 g; Total Fat: 33.49 g; Fiber: 0 g; Sugar: 0.2 g; Sodium: 217 mg; Potassium: 962 mg; Calcium (Ca): 40 mg; Vitamin B-12: 0.91 µg; Vitamin D: 47 IU

Creamy Cheese Chicken

Prep Time: 23 minutes | **Cook Time:** 45 minutes | **Serves:** 4

Ingredients:
4 chicken breasts, skinless, boneless & cut into chunks
1 cup light mayonnaise
1 teaspoon garlic powder
1 cup parmesan cheese, shredded
Pepper
Salt
Buttermilk to marinate

Directions:
Add chicken pieces into the bowl of buttermilk and soak overnight.
Set the oven's temperature 375 degrees F, timer for 45 minutes. Press start to preheat the oven.
Add marinated chicken pieces into the 9*13-inch baking dish. Mix together mayonnaise, garlic powder, ½ cup parmesan cheese, pepper, and salt and pour over chicken.
Drizzle remaining cheese on top of the chicken and bake for 40-45 minutes.
Serve and enjoy.

Per serving: Calories: 592; Carbs: 5.84 g; Protein: 67.07 g; Total Fat: 31.39 g; Fiber: 0.2 g; Sugar: 3.02 g; Sodium: 968 mg; Potassium: 1026 mg; Calcium (Ca): 294 mg; Vitamin B-12: 1.14 µg; Vitamin D: 6 IU

Homemade Chicken Meatballs

Prep Time: 12 minutes | **Cook Time:** 10 minutes | **Servings**: 4

Ingredients:
1-pound ground chicken
½ cup coconut flakes, crushed
1 tablespoon olive oil
1 teaspoon oregano, dried
1 egg, beaten
1 teaspoon minced garlic
1 teaspoon salt
½ teaspoon white pepper

Directions:
In the mixing bowl, mix up the chicken with other recipe ingredients except the oil; form medium meatballs from the mixture.
In the pan, heat the oil over medium heat; add the meatballs and cook them for 5 minutes on each side.
Serve and enjoy.

Per serving: Calories: 220; Carbs: 6.23 g; Protein: 26.99 g; Total Fat: 9.27 g; Fiber: 1.3 g; Sugar: 3.97 g; Sodium: 685 mg; Potassium: 350 mg; Calcium (Ca): 27 mg; Vitamin B-12: 0.54 µg; Vitamin D: 21 IU

Lemony Chicken Fillets

Prep Time: 10 minutes | **Cook Time:** 12 minutes | **Servings**: 4

Ingredients:
1 tablespoon lemon zest, grated
1 teaspoon olive oil
1 teaspoon turmeric powder
1 teaspoon lemon juice
½ teaspoon ground black pepper
1-pound chicken fillet, sliced

Directions:
In a large bowl, mix the chicken slices with other ingredients except for the oil.
In the pan, heat the oil over medium-high heat; add the chicken slices and cook them for 6 minutes on each side.
Serve.

Per serving: Calories: 142; Carbs: 1.39 g; Protein: 23.26 g; Total Fat: 4.23 g; Fiber: 0.3 g; Sugar: 0.44 g; Sodium: 86 mg; Potassium: 310 mg; Calcium (Ca): 14 mg; Vitamin B-12: 0.41 µg; Vitamin D: 12 IU

Broccoli Ranch Chicken

Prep Time: 15 minutes | **Cook Time:** 30 minutes | **Serves:** 4

Ingredients:
4 chicken breasts, skinless and boneless
⅓ cup mozzarella cheese, shredded
1 cup cheddar cheese, shredded
½ cup ranch dressing
5 bacon slices, cooked and chopped
2 cups broccoli florets, blanched and chopped

Directions:
Set the oven's temperature 375 degrees F, timer for 30 minutes. Press start to preheat the oven.
Add chicken into the 13*9-inch casserole dish. Top with bacon and broccoli.
Pour ranch dressing over chicken and top with shredded mozzarella cheese and cheddar cheese.
Bake chicken for 30 minutes.
Serve and enjoy.

Per serving: Calories: 447; Carbs: 11.75 g; Protein: 69.33 g; Total Fat: 12.12 g; Fiber: 0.9 g; Sugar: 3.71 g; Sodium: 853 mg; Potassium: 1070 mg; Calcium (Ca): 298 mg; Vitamin B-12: 0.99 µg; Vitamin D: 3 IU

Baked Chicken Breasts

Prep Time: 13 minutes | **Cook Time:** 20 minutes | **Serves:** 6

Ingredients:
6 chicken breasts, skinless & boneless
¼ teaspoon paprika
½ teaspoon garlic salt
1 teaspoon Italian seasoning
2 tablespoons olive oil
¼ teaspoon pepper

Directions:
Set temperature 390 degrees F, timer for 25 minutes. Press start to preheat the oven.
Brush chicken with oil. Mix together Italian seasoning, garlic salt, paprika, and pepper and rub all over the chicken.
Arrange chicken breasts on a roasting pan and bake for 25 minutes or until internal temperature reaches 165 degrees F.
Slice and serve.

Per serving: Calories: 369; Carbs: 0.59 g; Protein: 61.29 g; Total Fat: 11.64 g; Fiber: 0.1 g; Sugar: 0.16 g; Sodium: 158 mg; Potassium: 923 mg; Calcium (Ca): 15 mg; Vitamin B-12: 0.57 µg; Vitamin D: 3 IU

Simple Oregano Chicken Strips

Prep Time: 15 minutes | **Cook Time:** 10 minutes | **Servings**: 4

Ingredients:
1 teaspoon dried oregano
¼ teaspoon dried cilantro
¼ teaspoon nutmeg, ground
½ teaspoon ground paprika
½ teaspoon salt
1 tablespoon avocado oil
10 oz. chicken fillet, cut into strips

Directions:
In the pan, heat the avocado oil over medium-high heat; add the chicken strips and other ingredients, cook them for 10 minutes.
Serve.

Per serving: Calories: 219; Carbs: 1.93 g; Protein: 25.71 g; Total Fat: 11.52 g; Fiber: 0.6 g; Sugar: 0.34 g; Sodium: 111 mg; Potassium: 365 mg; Calcium (Ca): 38 mg; Vitamin B-12: 0.49 µg; Vitamin D: 0 IU

Chicken Greens Salad

Prep Time: 9 minutes | **Cook Time:** 0 | **Servings**: 4

Ingredients:
1 cup salad greens
1 tablespoons chives, chopped
1 tablespoons walnuts, chopped
1 tsp chili powder
1 tsp garlic powder
1 tablespoon olive oil
8 oz. chicken fillet, cubed and cooked
½ tsp salt

Directions:
In a salad bowl, mix all the ingredients and you can enjoy directly.

Per serving: Calories: 219; Carbs: 1.93 g; Protein: 25.71 g; Total Fat: 11.52 g; Fiber: 0.6 g; Sugar: 0.34 g; Sodium: 111 mg; Potassium: 365 mg; Calcium (Ca): 38 mg; Vitamin B-12: 0.49 µg; Vitamin D: 0 IU

Chicken Strips with Capers

Prep Time: 15 minutes | **Cook Time:** 10 minutes | **Servings**: 2

Ingredients:
¼ teaspoons cayenne pepper
¼ teaspoons salt
½ teaspoons turmeric powder
1 cup radishes, halved
¼ teaspoons minced garlic
1 tablespoon olive oil
1 tablespoon capers
8 oz. chicken fillet, boneless, skinless and cut into strips

Directions:
In the pan, heat the oil over medium heat.
Arrange the chicken strips in the hot oil in 1 layer and cook them for almost 3 minutes on each side; add other ingredients, stir and sauté for almost 4 minutes longer.
When done, serve.

Per serving: Calories: 135; Carbs: 0.44 g; Protein: 12.43 g; Total Fat: 9.34 g; Fiber: 0.2 g; Sugar: 0.05 g; Sodium: 334 mg; Potassium: 381 mg; Calcium (Ca): 9 mg; Vitamin B-12: 0.4 µg; Vitamin D: 8 IU

Almond Chicken Fillets

Prep Time: 10 minutes | **Cook Time:** 35 minutes | **Servings**: 4

Ingredients:
3 tablespoons reduced-fat mozzarella, shredded
1 tablespoon almonds
1 teaspoon olive oil
1 teaspoon turmeric powder
9 oz. chicken fillets, sliced
1 teaspoon salt
1 teaspoon ground black pepper
¼ cup of water

Directions:
In a roasting pan, mix the chicken fillets with other ingredients except for the cheese.
With the cheese on the top, bake the food in the oven at 370 degrees F for 35 minutes.

Per serving: Calories: 226; Carbs: 3.93 g; Protein: 38.19 g; Total Fat: 6.49 g; Fiber: 1.9 g; Sugar: 1.3 g; Sodium: 1250 mg; Potassium: 448 mg; Calcium (Ca): 825 mg; Vitamin B-12: 1.14 µg; Vitamin D: 7 IU

Chicken Breast and Mango

Prep Time: 25 minutes | **Cook Time:** 15 minutes | **Servings**: 4

Ingredients:
1 tablespoon chives, chopped
1 cup chicken breast, skinless, boneless, and cubed
½ cup mango, peeled and cubed
1 teaspoon dried oregano
1 teaspoon olive oil
1 tablespoon lime juice
½ teaspoon chili flakes

Directions:
In the pan, heat the oil over medium heat; add the chicken cubes and cook them for 5 minutes.
Add other ingredients and cook them for 10 minutes longer.
Serve and enjoy.

Per serving: Calories: 150; Carbs: 3.79 g; Protein: 15.4 g; Total Fat: 7.98 g; Fiber: 0.6 g; Sugar: 2.93 g; Sodium: 56 mg; Potassium: 211 mg; Calcium (Ca): 17 mg; Vitamin B-12: 0.25 µg; Vitamin D: 12 IU

Mustard Parmesan Turkey Breast

Prep Time: 10 minutes | **Cook Time:** 20 minutes | **Servings**: 4

Ingredients:
1-pound turkey breast, skinless, boneless, and cubed
1 tablespoon fat-free parmesan, grated
½ cup spring onions, chopped
1 tablespoon olive oil
A pinch of salt and black pepper
2 teaspoons mustard

Directions:
In the pan, heat the oil over medium heat; add the turkey breast cubes and cook for 10 minutes, stirring occasionally.
Add the resting ingredients and sauté for almost 10 minutes longer.
When done, serve.

Per serving: Calories: 219; Carbs: 1.93 g; Protein: 25.71 g; Total Fat: 11.52 g; Fiber: 0.6 g; Sugar: 0.34 g; Sodium: 111 mg; Potassium: 365 mg; Calcium (Ca): 38 mg; Vitamin B-12: 0.49 µg; Vitamin D: 0 IU

Chapter 3 Red Meat Recipes

Sautéed Lean Beef Steak with Onions

Prep Time: 15 minutes | **Cook Time:** 15 minutes | **Servings**: 2

Ingredients:
5 ounces' lean beef steak
1 small onion
1 small tomato, halved
1 cup spinach
1 teaspoon rosemary
1 teaspoon olive oil
Salt and black pepper to taste

Directions:
In the skillet, heat the oil and then sauté the onion until soft.
Add rosemary and sauté them until brown.
Add tomato and steak and cook them for 9 minutes, flipping the steaks halfway through.
Add spinach and cook for 3 minutes.
Serve warm.

Per serving: Calories: 154; Carbs: 7.78 g; Protein: 16.66 g; Total Fat: 6.41 g; Fiber: 1.9 g; Sugar: 3.89 g; Sodium: 58 mg; Potassium: 584 mg; Calcium (Ca): 35 mg; Vitamin B-12: 3.32 µg; Vitamin D: 0 IU

Mediterranean Beef and Rice

Prep Time: 15 minutes |**Cook Time:** 20 minutes | **Servings**: 4

Ingredients:
10 ounces' lean ground beef
½ cup rice, rinsed and drained
1 onion, chopped
1 garlic clove, minced
1 tablespoon olive oil
1 small tomato, chopped
1 teaspoon cumin
1 teaspoon coriander
1 teaspoon mint
1 teaspoon paprika
1 cup green beans

Directions:
In the skillet, heat the oil and sauté the beef for almost 3 minutes; add paprika, mint, coriander, cumin, garlic and onion, sauté then for 1 minute.
Add ⅓ cup of water, a pinch of salt and the rice.
Cover the skillet and simmer the food for 10 minutes.
When the time is up, stir in tomato and green beans, then cook until the rice is done.

Per serving: Calories: 197; Carbs: 13.32 g; Protein: 18.33 g; Total Fat: 10.32 g; Fiber: 4.8 g; Sugar: 2.97 g; Sodium: 53 mg; Potassium: 637 mg; Calcium (Ca): 40 mg; Vitamin B-12: 1.59 µg; Vitamin D: 2 IU

Rosemary Steak with Kale

Prep Time: 15 minutes | **Cook Time:** 15 minutes | **Serves:** 6

Ingredients:
3 garlic cloves, minced
2 tablespoons fresh rosemary, chopped
Salt and ground black pepper, as required
2 lbs. flank steak, trimmed
8 cups fresh baby kale

Directions:
Preheat the grill to medium-high heat.
Grease the grill grate.
In a suitable bowl, add all the ingredients except the steak and kale mix until well combined.
Add the steak and coat with the mixture generously.
Set aside for about 10 minutes.
Place the prepared steak onto the grill and cook for almost about 12-15 minutes, flipping after every 3-4 minutes.
Remove from the hot grill and place the steak onto a cutting board for about 5 minutes.
Meanwhile, for sauce: in a suitable bowl, add all the ingredients and mix well.
Serve the steak slices alongside the kale.

Per serving: Calories: 224; Carbs: 3.19 g; Protein: 33.58 g; Total Fat: 7.81 g; Fiber: 1 g; Sugar: 0.88 g; Sodium: 89 mg; Potassium: 656 mg; Calcium (Ca): 70 mg; Vitamin B-12: 1.38 µg; Vitamin D: 0 IU

Beef Broccoli

Prep Time: 15 minutes | **Cook Time:** 12 minutes | **Serves:** 1

Ingredients:
4 oz. lean ground beef
1 cup broccoli, cut into bite-sized pieces
2 tablespoons low-sodium chicken broth
¼ cup tomatoes, chopped
¼ teaspoon onion powder
¼ teaspoon garlic powder
Pinch of red pepper flakes
Salt, as required
1 oz. low-fat cheddar cheese

Directions:
Heat a lightly greased wok over medium heat and cook the beef for about 8-10 minutes or until browned completely.
Meanwhile, in a microwave-safe bowl, place the broccoli and broth.
With a plastic wrap, cover the bowl and microwave for about 4 minutes.
Remove from the microwave and set aside.
Drain the grease from wok.
Add the tomatoes, garlic powder, onion powder, red pepper flakes, and salt and stir to combine well.
Stir in broccoli and toss to coat well.
Remove from the heat and transfer the beef mixture into a serving bowl.
Top with cheddar cheese and serve.

Per serving: Calories: 280; Carbs: 8.46 g; Protein: 35.58 g; Total Fat: 12.36 g; Fiber: 2.4 g; Sugar: 3.69 g; Sodium: 480 mg; Potassium: 776 mg; Calcium (Ca): 270 mg; Vitamin B-12: 2.81 µg; Vitamin D: 8 IU

Pork Broccoli Fry

Prep Time: 15 minutes | **Cook Time:** 15 minutes | **Serves:** 4

Ingredients:
1-pound pork loin, cut into thin strips
2 tablespoons olive oil,
1 teaspoon garlic, minced
1 teaspoon fresh ginger, minced
2 tablespoons low-sodium soy sauce
1 tablespoon fresh lemon juice
1 tablespoon Erythritol
1 teaspoon arrowroot starch
10 oz. broccoli florets
1 carrot, peeled and sliced
1 red bell pepper, cut into strips
2 scallions, cut into 2-inch pieces

Directions:
In a suitable bowl, mix well pork strips, ½ tablespoon of olive oil, garlic, and ginger.
For sauce; add the soy sauce, lemon juice, erythritol, and arrowroot starch in a small bowl and mix well.
Heat the remaining oil in a suitable nonstick wok over high heat and sear the pork strips for almost 3-4 minutes or until cooked through.
With a slotted spoon, transfer the pork into a suitable bowl.
In the same wok, add the carrot and cook for almost about 2-3 minutes.
Add the broccoli, bell pepper, and scallion and cook, covered for about 1-2 minutes.
Stir the cooked pork and sauce, and cook for almost about 3-5 minutes or until desired doneness, stirring occasionally.
Remove from the heat and serve.

Per serving: Calories: 251; Carbs: 7.91 g; Protein: 28.72 g; Total Fat: 11.81 g; Fiber: 2.4 g; Sugar: 3.69 g; Sodium: 345 mg; Potassium: 656 mg; Calcium (Ca): 93 mg; Vitamin B-12: 0.58 µg; Vitamin D: 18 IU

Italian Lean Beef Meatballs

Prep Time: 15 minutes |**Cook Time:** 12 minutes | **Servings**: 4

Ingredients:
1-pound ground beef, lean
1 teaspoon minced garlic
1 teaspoon oregano, dried
1 teaspoon Italian seasoning
1 teaspoon ground paprika
1 teaspoon salt
1 teaspoon dried parsley
1 tablespoon olive oil

Directions:
In a suitable bowl, mix up all the recipe ingredients except for the oil, then shape medium meatballs out of the mixture.
In the pan, heat the oil over medium heat; add meatballs and cook them for 6 minutes on each side.
Serve.

Per serving: Calories: 184; Carbs: 1.16 g; Protein: 24.47 g; Total Fat: 9.14 g; Fiber: 0.4 g; Sugar: 0.16 g; Sodium: 709 mg; Potassium: 421 mg; Calcium (Ca): 18 mg; Vitamin B-12: 2.54 µg; Vitamin D: 3 IU

Beef Chili

Prep Time: 15 minutes | **Cook Time:** 1 hour 45 minutes | **Serves:** 8

Ingredients:
2 tablespoons olive oil
3 lbs. ground beef
1 cup yellow onion, chopped
½ cup celery, chopped
½ cup green bell pepper, seeded and chopped
½ cup red bell pepper, seeded and chopped
1 (15-oz.) can crushed tomatoes with juice
1½ cups tomato juice
1½ teaspoons Worcestershire sauce
½ teaspoon dried oregano
3 tablespoons red chili powder
1 teaspoon ground cumin
1 teaspoon garlic powder
1 teaspoon salt
½ teaspoon ground black pepper

Directions:
In a suitable pan, heat the oil over medium-high heat and cook the beef for about 8-10 minutes or until browned.
Drain the grease from pan, leaving about 2 tablespoons inside.
In this pan, add the onions, celery, and bell peppers over medium-high heat and cook for almost about 5 minutes, stirring frequently.
Add the tomatoes, tomato juice, Worcestershire sauce, oregano and spices and stir to combine.
Reduce its heat to low and simmer, covered for about 1-1½ hours, stirring occasionally.
Serve hot.

Per serving: Calories: 303; Carbs: 8.48 g; Protein: 38.26 g; Total Fat: 13.85 g; Fiber: 3.6 g; Sugar: 4.36 g; Sodium: 621 mg; Potassium: 950 mg; Calcium (Ca): 72 mg; Vitamin B-12: 3.81 µg; Vitamin D: 5 IU

Colombian Lean Beef Sirloin Steaks

Prep Time: 10 minutes | **Cook Time:** 30 minutes | **Servings**: 2

Ingredients:
10 oz. lean beef sirloin steaks
1 carrot, peeled and sliced
1 garlic clove, diced
½ teaspoon ground coriander
2 teaspoons lemon juice
1 tablespoon fresh parsley, chopped
1 tablespoon olive oil
⅓ cup water

Directions:
In the skillet, heat the olive oil; add the steaks and cook them for 5 minutes on each side.
Transfer the steaks to the baking pan and add other ingredients, then roast then for 20 minutes over medium heat.
Divide between plates and serve.

Per serving: Calories: 332; Carbs: 1.12 g; Protein: 29.5 g; Total Fat: 22.57 g; Fiber: 0.2 g; Sugar: 0.23 g; Sodium: 78 mg; Potassium: 482 mg; Calcium (Ca): 44 mg; Vitamin B-12: 1.39 µg; Vitamin D: 0 IU

Garlicky Pork Tenderloin

Prep Time: 10 minutes | **Cook Time:** 38 minutes | **Serves:** 6

Ingredients:
3 medium garlic cloves, minced
3 teaspoons dried rosemary, crushed
½ teaspoon cayenne pepper
Salt and ground black pepper, as required
2 lbs. pork tenderloin
10 cups fresh baby spinach

Directions:
At 400 degrees F, preheat your oven.
Grease a suitable roasting pan.
In a suitable bowl, mix all the recipe ingredients except for pork and spinach.
Rub the pork with this garlic mixture evenly.
Place the pork into the prepared pan.
Cook for almost 25 minutes or until done.
Remove the roasting pan from oven and place the pork tenderloin onto a cutting board for about 10-15 minutes.
With a sharp knife, cut the pork tenderloin into desired size slices and serve alongside spinach.

Per serving: Calories: 180; Carbs: 2.71 g; Protein: 33.27 g; Total Fat: 3.54 g; Fiber: 1.3 g; Sugar: 0.24 g; Sodium: 120 mg; Potassium: 899 mg; Calcium (Ca): 63 mg; Vitamin B-12: 0.77 µg; Vitamin D: 12 IU

Beef with Mushrooms

Prep Time: 15 minutes | **Cook Time:** 15 minutes | **Serves:** 4

Ingredients:
For Beef:
4 (6-oz.) beef tenderloin fillets
Salt and black pepper, to taste
2 tablespoons olive oil,
1 teaspoon garlic, smashed
1 tablespoon fresh thyme, chopped
For Mushrooms:
2 tablespoons olive oil
1 pound fresh mushrooms, sliced
2 teaspoons garlic, smashed
Salt and black pepper, to taste

Directions:
For beef: season the beef fillets with salt and black pepper evenly and set aside.
In a cast-iron wok, heat the oil over medium heat and sauté the garlic and thyme for about 1 minute.
Add the fillets and cook for almost 5-7 minutes per side.
Meanwhile, for mushrooms: in another cast-iron wok, heat the oil over medium heat and cook the mushrooms, garlic, salt, and black pepper for about 7-8 minutes, stirring frequently.
Divide the fillets onto serving plates.
Top with mushroom mixture and serve.

Per serving: Calories: 266; Carbs: 4.92 g; Protein: 11.45 g; Total Fat: 23.21 g; Fiber: 1.4 g; Sugar: 2.27 g; Sodium: 27 mg; Potassium: 510 mg; Calcium (Ca): 15 mg; Vitamin B-12: 1.15 µg; Vitamin D: 8 IU

Sirloin Steak with Broccoli

Prep Time: 15 minutes | **Cook Time:** 20 minutes | **Servings:** 6

Ingredients:
16 ounces of sirloin steak, trimmed and cut into thin strips
Salt and black pepper, to taste
2 tablespoons of olive oil, divided
2 garlic cloves, minced
1 Serrano pepper, seeded and chopped
2 cups of broccoli florets
2 tablespoons of low-sodium soy sauce
2 tablespoons of fresh lime juice

Directions:
Season the steak strips with black pepper.
In the skillet, heat 1 tablespoon of oil over medium heat and then cook the steak strips for 6 to 8 minutes, or until browned from all sides.
Transfer the steak slices onto a suitable plate.
Still in the skillet, heat the remaining oil over medium heat; sauté the garlic and Serrano pepper for 1 minute.
Add the broccoli and sauté for about 2 to 3 minutes; put the steak strips back and add the soy sauce and lime juice, cook them for 3 to 4 minutes.
Serve hot.

Per serving: Calories: 133; Carbs: 1.71 g; Protein: 16.26 g; Total Fat: 6.56 g; Fiber: 0.6 g; Sugar: 0.21 g; Sodium: 236 mg; Potassium: 324 mg; Calcium (Ca): 29 mg; Vitamin B-12: 1.01 µg; Vitamin D: 0 IU

Ground Beef Fry

Prep Time: 15 minutes | **Cook Time:** 25 minutes | **Serves:** 4

Ingredients:
1-pound lean ground beef
2 tablespoons extra-virgin olive oil
2 garlic cloves, minced
½ of yellow onion, chopped
2 cups fresh mushrooms, sliced
1 cup fresh kale, tough ribs removed and chopped
¼ cup low-sodium beef broth
2 tablespoons balsamic vinegar
2 tablespoons fresh parsley, chopped

Directions:
Heat a suitable non-stick wok over medium-high heat and cook the ground beef for about 8-10 minutes.
With a slotted spoon, transfer the beef into a suitable bowl.
In the same wok, stir in onion and garlic for about 3 minutes.
Add the mushrooms and cook for almost about 5-minutes.
Add the cooked beef, kale, broth and vinegar and cook to a boil.
Then reduce its heat to medium-low and simmer for about 3 minutes.
Stir in parsley and serve immediately.

Per serving: Calories: 299; Carbs: 5.21 g; Protein: 31.5 g; Total Fat: 16.03 g; Fiber: 0.5 g; Sugar: 2.09 g; Sodium: 138 mg; Potassium: 439 mg; Calcium (Ca): 34 mg; Vitamin B-12: 2.87 µg; Vitamin D: 2 IU

Beef Taco Meal

Prep Time: 15 minutes | **Cook Time:** 15 minutes | **Serves:** 4

Ingredients:
1 teaspoon red chili powder
1 teaspoon ground cumin
Salt and black pepper, to taste
1-pound flank steak, trimmed
2 scallions
1 lime, cut in half
8 cups lettuce, torn
1 red bell pepper, seeded and sliced
1 cup tomato, chopped
½ cup fresh cilantro, chopped
¼ cup light sour cream

Directions:
Preheat the grill to medium-high heat. Grease the grill grate.
In a suitable bowl, mix the spices with salt and black pepper.
Rub the steak with spice mixture generously.
Set the steak onto the grill and cook for almost about 4-6 minutes per side or until desired doneness.
Remove from the hot grill and place the steak onto a cutting board for about 5 minutes.
Now, place the scallions onto the grill and cook for almost about 1 minute per side.
Place the lime halves onto the grill, cut-side down and cook for almost about 1 minute.
Remove the scallions and lime halves from the grill and place onto a plate.
Chop the scallions roughly.
In a suitable bowl, place the beef slices and chopped scallions.
Squeeze the lime halves over steak mixture and toss to coat well.
Divide lettuce into serving bowls and top each with bell pepper, followed by tomato, cilantro and beef mixture.
Top each bowl with sour cream and serve.

Per serving: Calories: 215; Carbs: 9.15 g; Protein: 27.41 g; Total Fat: 7.84 g; Fiber: 2.6 g; Sugar: 3.88 g; Sodium: 146 mg; Potassium: 900 mg; Calcium (Ca): 105 mg; Vitamin B-12: 1.09 µg; Vitamin D: 1 IU

Juicy Steak

Prep Time: 10 minutes | **Cook Time:** 10 minutes | **Serves:** 4

Ingredients:
1 tablespoon olive oil
4 (6-oz.) flank steaks
Salt and ground black pepper, as required
6 cups fresh salad greens

Directions:
In a wok, preheat the oil over medium-high heat and cook steaks with salt and black pepper for about 3-5 minutes per side.
Transfer the grilled steaks onto serving plates and serve alongside the greens.

Per serving: Calories: 103; Carbs: 3.11 g; Protein: 10.08 g; Total Fat: 5.65 g; Fiber: 1.9 g; Sugar: 0.88 g; Sodium: 43 mg; Potassium: 366 mg; Calcium (Ca): 54 mg; Vitamin B-12: 0.39 µg; Vitamin D: 0 IU

Veggie Stuffed Steak

Prep Time: 15 minutes | **Cook Time:** 35 minutes | **Servings:** 6

Ingredients:
1 (1½-pound) flank steak
Salt and black pepper, to taste
1 tablespoon of olive oil
2 small garlic cloves, minced
6 ounces of fresh spinach, chopped
1 green bell pepper, seeded and diced
1 tomato, chopped

Directions:
Preheat the oven to 425 degrees F. Grease a large baking dish.
Place beefsteak onto a flat surface.
Hold a pointy knife parallel to figure surface, slice the steak horizontally, without cutting all the way through, that you simply can open sort of a book.
Use a meat mallet to flatten the steak to a good thickness.
Sprinkle the steak with salt and black pepper evenly.
In the skillet, heat the oil over medium heat and sauté garlic for about 1 minute; add the spinach, salt, black pepper and sauté them for 2 minutes.
Stir in bell pepper and tomato and immediately remove from heat.
Transfer the spinach into a bowl and put aside to chill slightly.
Place the filling on the top of steak evenly, roll up the steak to seal the filling and then tie the steak with cotton twine.
Place the steak roll into the prepared baking dish and then roast the food in the oven for 30 to 35 minutes.
Remove it from the hot oven and let it cool slightly.
With a pointy knife, cut the roll into desired sized slices and serve.

Per serving: Calories: 76; Carbs: 3.32 g; Protein: 7.44 g; Total Fat: 3.89 g; Fiber: 1.3 g; Sugar: 1.15 g; Sodium: 40 mg; Potassium: 349 mg; Calcium (Ca): 42 mg; Vitamin B-12: 0.26 µg; Vitamin D: 0 IU

Lean Beef and Eggplant

Prep Time: 10 minutes | **Cook Time:** 20 minutes | **Servings:** 2

Ingredients:
1-pound lean beef fillet, cut into strips
1 cup eggplant, cubed
½ cup crushed tomatoes
1 tablespoon avocado oil
1 teaspoon salt
1 teaspoon black pepper
1 teaspoon fresh rosemary

Directions:
In the pan, heat the oil over medium heat; add the beef strips and cook for 5 minutes.
Add other recipe ingredients and cook for 15 minutes longer.
Divide the food into bowls and enjoy.

Per serving: Calories: 385; Carbs: 4.86 g; Protein: 47.43 g; Total Fat: 20.17 g; Fiber: 2.1 g; Sugar: 2.44 g; Sodium: 1361 mg; Potassium: 1095 mg; Calcium (Ca): 59 mg; Vitamin B-12: 6.76 µg; Vitamin D: 7 IU

Beef Tenderloin Fillets and Mushrooms

Prep Time: 15 minutes | **Cook Time:** 15 minutes | **Servings:** 6

Ingredients:
For Beef:
4 (6-ounces) beef tenderloin fillets
Salt and black pepper, to taste
2 tablespoons of olive oil, divided
1 teaspoon of garlic, smashed
1 tablespoon of fresh thyme, chopped
For Mushrooms:
2 tablespoons of olive oil
1-pound fresh mushrooms, sliced
2 teaspoons of garlic, smashed
Salt and black pepper, to taste

Directions:
To make the beef:
Season the beef fillets with salt and black pepper evenly. Set aside.
In a cast-iron skillet, heat the oil over medium heat; sauté the garlic and thyme for 1 minute.
Add the fillets and cook for about 5 to 7 minutes on each side.
To make the mushroom:
In another cast-iron skillet, heat the oil over medium heat and sauté the mushrooms, garlic, salt, and black pepper for 7 to 8 minutes.
Divide the fillets onto serving plates, top with mushroom mixture and serve.

Per serving: Calories: 355; Carbs: 58.53 g; Protein: 13.79 g; Total Fat: 11.8 g; Fiber: 9 g; Sugar: 2.22 g; Sodium: 55 mg; Potassium: 1290 mg; Calcium (Ca): 23 mg; Vitamin B-12: 0.34 µg; Vitamin D: 116 IU

Lean Lamb Burgers

Prep Time: 15 minutes | **Cook Time:** 15 minutes | **Servings:** 2

Ingredients:
8 ounces ground lamb, lean
½ teaspoon chili powder
½ teaspoon salt
½ teaspoon sweet paprika
¼ teaspoon turmeric powder
1 tablespoon chives, chopped
1 tablespoon olive oil

Directions:
In a suitable bowl, mix the lamb with other recipe ingredients except the oil; shape 2 burgers out of this mixture.
In the pan, heat the oil over medium-high heat; add burgers and cook for almost 6 minutes on each side.
Serve and enjoy.

Per serving: Calories: 284; Carbs: 1.01 g; Protein: 23.32 g; Total Fat: 21.02 g; Fiber: 0.6 g; Sugar: 0.15 g; Sodium: 667 mg; Potassium: 359 mg; Calcium (Ca): 11 mg; Vitamin B-12: 1.84 µg; Vitamin D: 1 IU

Sirloin Steaks with Green Beans

Prep Time: 15 minutes | **Cook Time:** 10 minutes | **Servings:** 6

Ingredients:
For Steak:
2 (5-ounces) sirloin steaks, trimmed
Salt and ground black pepper, as required
1 tablespoon of extra-virgin olive oil
1 garlic clove, minced
For Green Beans:
½ pound fresh green beans
½ tablespoon of olive oil
½ tablespoon of fresh lemon juice

Directions:
To make the steaks:
Season the steaks with salt and black pepper evenly.
In a pan, heat the vegetable oil over high heat and sauté garlic for about 15 to 20 seconds.
Add the steaks and cook them for 3 to 4 minutes on each side, or until they reach the doneness that you like.
To make the green beans:
In another suitable pan, boil the water and then arrange a steamer basket in it.
Place the green beans in the prepared steamer basket and cover them, steam them for about 4 to 5 minutes.
Carefully transfer the beans into a bowl.
Add vegetable oil and juice and toss to coat well.
Divide green beans onto serving plates, top each with 1 steak and serve.

Per serving: Calories: 59; Carbs: 3.13 g; Protein: 5.55 g; Total Fat: 2.85 g; Fiber: 1.1 g; Sugar: 1.27 g; Sodium: 41 mg; Potassium: 171 mg; Calcium (Ca): 19 mg; Vitamin B-12: 0.32 µg; Vitamin D: 0 IU

Coffee Lean Skirt Steaks

Prep Time: 15 minutes | **Cook Time:** 25 minutes | **Servings:** 4

Ingredients:
½ tablespoon ground Coffee
1 teaspoon nutmeg, ground
½ teaspoon salt
1 teaspoon sweet paprika
1-pound lean skirt steak, sliced
1 tablespoon olive oil

Directions:
Preheat the oven to 380 degrees F. Line the baking pan with parchment paper.
In a bowl, mix up the steaks with other recipe ingredients except the oil.
Arrange the steaks and grease them with the oil, then cook them in the oven for 25 minutes.
When done, serve and enjoy.

Per serving: Calories: 197; Carbs: 0.58 g; Protein: 24.25 g; Total Fat: 10.99 g; Fiber: 0.3 g; Sugar: 0.08 g; Sodium: 374 mg; Potassium: 456 mg; Calcium (Ca): 20 mg; Vitamin B-12: 3.4 µg; Vitamin D: 5 IU

Steak with Green Beans

Prep Time: 15 minutes | **Cook Time:** 10 minutes | **Serves:** 2

Ingredients:
For Steak:
2 (5-oz.) sirloin steaks, trimmed
Salt and ground black pepper, as required
1 tablespoon extra-virgin olive oil
1 garlic clove, minced
For Green Beans:
½ pound fresh green beans
½ tablespoon olive oil
½ tablespoon fresh lemon juice

Directions:
For steak: season the steaks with salt and black pepper evenly.
In a cast-iron sauté pan, heat the olive oil over high heat and sauté garlic for about 15-20 seconds.
Add the steaks and cook for almost about 3 minutes per side.
Flip the steaks and cook for almost about 3-4 minutes or until desired doneness, flipping once.
Meanwhile, for green beans: in a suitable pan of boiling water, arrange a steamer basket.
Place the green beans in steamer basket and steam, covered for about 4-5 minutes.
Carefully transfer the beans into a suitable bowl.
Drizzle lemon juice and olive oil on top of the beans and toss to coat well.
Divide green beans onto serving plates.
Top each with 1 steak and serve.

Per serving: Calories: 176; Carbs: 9.4 g; Protein: 16.65 g; Total Fat: 8.54 g; Fiber: 3.4 g; Sugar: 3.81 g; Sodium: 124 mg; Potassium: 514 mg; Calcium (Ca): 58 mg; Vitamin B-12: 0.96 µg; Vitamin D: 0 IU

Garlicky Lean Pork Ribs

Prep Time: 20 minutes | **Cook Time:** 25 minutes | **Servings:** 4

Ingredients:
16 oz. lean pork spare ribs, chopped
½ cup spring onions, chopped
4 tablespoons balsamic vinegar
1 teaspoon chili powder
1 tablespoon olive oil
1 garlic clove, diced

Directions:
In the mixing bowl, mix up the pork ribs with other recipe ingredients; marinate the meat for 15 to 20 minutes.
In the skillet, cook the marinated pork ribs over medium heat for 7 minutes on each side.
Cove the skillet, reduce the heat to low and then cook them for 10 minutes longer.
When done, serve and enjoy.

Per serving: Calories: 210; Carbs: 4.23 g; Protein: 23.99 g; Total Fat: 9.89 g; Fiber: 0.6 g; Sugar: 2.74 g; Sodium: 101 mg; Potassium: 452 mg; Calcium (Ca): 41 mg; Vitamin B-12: 1.15 µg; Vitamin D: 25 IU

Pork Veggie Burgers

Prep Time: 15 minutes | **Cook Time:** 16 minutes | **Serves:** 4

Ingredients:
For Patties:
1-pound ground pork
1 carrot, peeled and chopped
1 raw beetroot, peeled and chopped
1 small onion, chopped
2 Serrano peppers, seeded and chopped
1 tablespoon fresh cilantro, chopped
Salt and ground black pepper, as required
3 tablespoons olive oil
For Serves:
1 large onion, sliced
2 large tomatoes, sliced
4 lettuce leaves

Directions:
For patties: in a suitable bowl, add all ingredients except for oil and mix until well mixed.
Make equal-sized 8 patties from this pork mixture.
In a suitable non-stick sauté pan, preheat the olive oil over medium heat and cook the patties for almost 3-4 minutes per side.
Divide the onion, tomato and lettuce onto serving plates.
Add 2 prepared patties on top of each plate and enjoy.

Per serving: Calories: 268; Carbs: 9.78 g; Protein: 25.26 g; Total Fat: 14.85 g; Fiber: 2.3 g; Sugar: 4.81 g; Sodium: 106 mg; Potassium: 595 mg; Calcium (Ca): 44 mg; Vitamin B-12: 0.73 µg; Vitamin D: 5 IU

Coriander Lean Lamb Chops

Prep Time: 25 minutes | **Cook Time:** 15 minutes | **Servings**: 4

Ingredients:
4 lean lamb chops
1 teaspoon ground coriander
½ teaspoon sweet paprika
A pinch of black pepper
1 teaspoon salt
1 teaspoon chili powder
1 tablespoon olive oil

Directions:
In the mixing bowl, mix up lamb chops with other recipe ingredients and let the meat sit for 25 minutes to 25 minutes.
Preheat the grill to 385 degrees F.
Place the lamb chops on the preheated grill and cook them for almost 7 minutes on each side.
When done, serve and enjoy.

Per serving: Calories: 329; Carbs: 0.87 g; Protein: 15.7 g; Total Fat: 28.83 g; Fiber: 0.5 g; Sugar: 0.08 g; Sodium: 654 mg; Potassium: 231 mg; Calcium (Ca): 20 mg; Vitamin B-12: 1.94 µg; Vitamin D: 0 IU

Pork Burgers

Prep Time: 15 minutes | **Cook Time:** 6 minutes | **Serves:** 4

Ingredients:
For Patties:
1-pound lean ground pork
¼ cup fresh parsley, chopped
¼ cup fresh cilantro, chopped
1 tablespoon fresh ginger, chopped
1 teaspoon ground cumin
1 teaspoon ground coriander
½ teaspoon ground cinnamon
Salt and ground black pepper, as required
For Salad:
6 cups fresh baby arugula
2 cups cherry tomatoes, quartered
1 tablespoon fresh lemon juice
1 tablespoon extra-virgin olive oil

Directions:
In a suitable bowl, add the pork, parsley, cilantro, ginger, spices, salt and black pepper and mix until well combined.
Make 4 equal-sized patties from the mixture.
Heat a suitable grill pan over medium-high heat and cook the patties for about 3 minutes per side or until desired doneness.
Meanwhile, in a suitable bowl, add arugula, tomatoes, lemon juice and oil and toss to coat well.
Divide the prepared salad onto serving plates and top each with 1 patty.
Serve immediately.

Per serving: Calories: 183; Carbs: 6.6 g; Protein: 25.88 g; Total Fat: 6.58 g; Fiber: 2 g; Sugar: 3.33 g; Sodium: 122 mg; Potassium: 726 mg; Calcium (Ca): 89 mg; Vitamin B-12: 0.73 µg; Vitamin D: 5 IU

Chapter 4 Fish and Seafood Recipes

Lettuce Seafood Wraps

Prep Time: 10 minutes | **Cook Time:** 0 | **Servings**: 6

Ingredients:
6 lettuce leaves
8 oz. salmon, canned
4 oz. crab meat, canned
1 cucumber
2 tablespoons Plain yogurt
½ teaspoon minced garlic
1 tablespoon fresh dill, chopped
¼ teaspoon tarragon

Directions:
Grate the cucumber with a grater.
In a suitable bowl, mash the salmon and crab meat; add the yogurt, minced garlic, fresh dill, tarragon and the grated cucumber, mix them well.
Fill the lettuce leaves with the cooked mixture and then you can enjoy.

Per serving: Calories: 85; Carbs: 1.77 g; Protein: 11.82 g; Total Fat: 3.24 g; Fiber: 0.5 g; Sugar: 0.75 g; Sodium: 242 mg; Potassium: 254 mg; Calcium (Ca): 122 mg; Vitamin B-12: 0.8 µg; Vitamin D: 288 IU

Mango Tilapia Fillets

Prep Time: 10 minutes | **Cook Time:** 15 minutes | **Servings**: 4

Ingredients:
¼ cup coconut flakes
5 oz. mango, peeled
⅓ cup shallot, chopped
1 teaspoon ground turmeric
1 cup of water
1 bay leaf
12 oz. tilapia fillets
1 chili pepper, chopped
1 tablespoon coconut oil
½ teaspoon salt
1 teaspoon paprika

Directions:
Sprinkle the salt and paprika over the tilapia fillets.
In a blender, add the coconut flakes, mango, shallot, ground turmeric, water and blend them well.
In the saucepan, heat the coconut oil; place in the fillets and then roast them for 1 minute on each side.
Add chili pepper, bay leaf, and blended mango mixture.
Cover the pan and cook the food for 10 minutes over medium heat.
When done, serve and enjoy.

Per serving: Calories: 170; Carbs: 11.03 g; Protein: 18.07 g; Total Fat: 6.61 g; Fiber: 1.9 g; Sugar: 7.91 g; Sodium: 354 mg; Potassium: 423 mg; Calcium (Ca): 27 mg; Vitamin B-12: 1.34 µg; Vitamin D: 105 IU

Cod and Egg Sandwiches

Prep Time: 10 minutes | **Cook Time:** 10 minutes | **Servings**: 4

Ingredients:
2 (5 ounce) can cod, drained 6 hard-cooked eggs, peeled and chopped
2 cups chopped celery
2 tablespoons low-fat mayonnaise
Pepper to taste
8 slices white bread

Directions:
In a suitable bowl, mix the cod with the eggs, celery, mayonnaise and pepper.
Place ¼ of the mixture onto one slice of bread and cover with another bread slice.
Do the same with the remaining mixture and bread slices.
Serve and enjoy.

Per serving: Calories: 321; Carbs: 27.23 g; Protein: 41.85 g; Total Fat: 3.98 g; Fiber: 6 g; Sugar: 3.77 g; Sodium: 656 mg; Potassium: 1027 mg; Calcium (Ca): 436 mg; Vitamin B-12: 1.64 µg; Vitamin D: 73 IU

Grilled Shrimp

Prep Time: 12 -15 minutes | **Cook Time:** 10 minutes | **Serves:** 2

Ingredients:
8 oz. shrimp, deveined
1 teaspoon sweet paprika
1 teaspoon lemon juice
1 teaspoon olive oil
½ teaspoon chives, chopped

Directions:
At 375 degrees F, preheat your grill.
In a suitable mixing bowl, put the shrimp with the rest of the ingredients, toss, place on the grill, and cook for almost 5 minutes.

Per serving: Calories: 120; Carbs: 0.81 g; Protein: 22.97 g; Total Fat: 2.98 g; Fiber: 0.4 g; Sugar: 0.19 g; Sodium: 136 mg; Potassium: 329 mg; Calcium (Ca): 76 mg; Vitamin B-12: 0 µg; Vitamin D: 50 IU

Indian Spiced Cod

Prep Time: 9 minutes | **Cook Time:** 20 minutes | **Serves:** 2

Ingredients:
16 oz. cod fillets
2 teaspoons garam masala
¼ cup almond milk
A pinch of salt and black pepper
1 teaspoon olive oil

Directions:
Preheat your oven to 365 degrees F.
Brush the baking pan with olive oil.
Combine all the ingredients in the pan.
Cook the cod in the preheated oven at 365 degrees F for 20 minutes.

Per serving: Calories: 207; Carbs: 6.18 g; Protein: 35.6 g; Total Fat: 3.9 g; Fiber: 1.3 g; Sugar: 4.01 g; Sodium: 712 mg; Potassium: 684 mg; Calcium (Ca): 84 mg; Vitamin B-12: 4.87 µg; Vitamin D: 58 IU

Thyme Shrimp

Prep Time: 9 minutes | **Cook Time:** 6 minutes | **Serves:** 2

Ingredients:
1-pound shrimp, peeled and deveined
1 teaspoon dried thyme
1 teaspoon lime juice
2 teaspoons olive oil
¼ teaspoon salt

Directions:
Heat a suitable pan with the oil over medium heat, add the shrimp and the other ingredients, cook for almost 6 minutes and serve.

Per serving: Calories: 234; Carbs: 0.31 g; Protein: 45.62 g; Total Fat: 5.67 g; Fiber: 0.1 g; Sugar: 0.04 g; Sodium: 561 mg; Potassium: 604 mg; Calcium (Ca): 147 mg; Vitamin B-12: 0 µg; Vitamin D: 0 IU

Shrimp Mix

Prep Time: 9 minutes | **Cook Time:** 14 minutes | **Serves:** 4

Ingredients:
2-pound shrimps, peeled and deveined
1 teaspoon lime juice
1 teaspoon chili powder
1 tablespoon olive oil
½ teaspoon ground nutmeg
2 tablespoons water

Directions:
At 360 degrees F, preheat your oven.
Layer a suitable baking tray with the baking paper.
Arrange the shrimps in the baking tray in one layer. Add the resting ingredients, toss and cook them for 14 minutes.
Flip the shrimps on another side after 7 minutes of cooking.

Per serving: Calories: 226; Carbs: 0.58 g; Protein: 45.7 g; Total Fat: 4.73 g; Fiber: 0.3 g; Sugar: 0.08 g; Sodium: 290 mg; Potassium: 614 mg; Calcium (Ca): 149 mg; Vitamin B-12: 0 µg; Vitamin D: 0 IU

Limey Trout Fillets

Prep Time: 9 minutes | **Cook Time:** 12 minutes | **Serves:** 6

Ingredients:
6 trout fillets, boneless
½ cup fresh cilantro, chopped
3 tablespoons olive oil
1 tablespoon lime juice
1 teaspoon chili powder
½ teaspoon salt

Directions:
Heat a suitable pan with the oil over medium-high heat, add the trout and the other ingredients, cook for almost 6 minutes on each side and serve.

Per serving: Calories: 251; Carbs: 0.48 g; Protein: 32.66 g; Total Fat: 12.32 g; Fiber: 0.2 g; Sugar: 0.09 g; Sodium: 257 mg; Potassium: 784 mg; Calcium (Ca): 109 mg; Vitamin B-12: 7.08 µg; Vitamin D: 422 IU

Fish Chili with Lentils

Prep Time: 10 minutes | **Cook Time:** 30 minutes | **Servings:** 4

Ingredients:
1 red pepper, chopped
1 yellow onion, diced
1 teaspoon ground black pepper
1 teaspoon butter
1 jalapeno pepper, chopped
½ cup lentils
3 cups chicken stock
1 teaspoon salt
1 tablespoon tomato paste
1 teaspoon chili pepper
3 tablespoons fresh cilantro, chopped
8 oz. cod, chopped

Directions:
In the saucepan over medium heat, cook the butter, red pepper, onion and ground black pepper for 5 minutes.
Add chopped jalapeno pepper, lentils, and chili pepper, mix the prepared mixture well and add chicken stock and tomato paste; stir until homogenous.
Add cod and then cover the pan.
Cook the food for 20 minutes.
When done, serve and enjoy.

Per serving: Calories: 95; Carbs: 9.05 g; Protein: 11.76 g; Total Fat: 1.79 g; Fiber: 1.4 g; Sugar: 3.78 g; Sodium: 1460 mg; Potassium: 376 mg; Calcium (Ca): 376 mg; Vitamin B-12: 1.16 µg; Vitamin D: 12 IU

Tuna Casserole

Prep Time: 15 minutes | **Cook Time:** 35 minutes | **Servings:** 4

Ingredients:
½ cup Cheddar cheese, shredded
2 tomatoes, chopped
7 oz. tuna filet, chopped
1 teaspoon ground coriander
½ teaspoon salt
1 teaspoon olive oil
½ teaspoon dried oregano

Directions:
Brush the casserole mold with olive oil.
Mix the chopped tuna fillet with dried oregano and ground coriander.
Place the fish in the mold and flatten well to get the layer, then add the chopped tomatoes and shredded cheese.
Cover the casserole with foil and secure the edges.
Bake the meal in the oven at 355 degrees F for 35 minutes.
When done, serve and enjoy.

Per serving: Calories: 100; Carbs: 4 g; Protein: 14.56 g; Total Fat: 2.76 g; Fiber: 0.8 g; Sugar: 2.62 g; Sodium: 472 mg; Potassium: 402 mg; Calcium (Ca): 89 mg; Vitamin B-12: 1.2 µg; Vitamin D: 34 IU

Lemon Cod Fillets

Prep Time: 20 minutes | **Cook Time:** 30 minutes | **Servings**: 5

Ingredients:
½ cup butter
1 lemon, juiced
1 teaspoon ground black pepper
½ teaspoon dried basil
3 cloves garlic, minced
6 (4 ounce) fillets cod
2 tablespoons lemon pepper

Directions:
At 350 degrees F, preheat your oven.
In the saucepan, melt the butter over medium heat and bring to a boil.
Place the cleaned cod fillets in a single layer on a suitable baking sheet.
Cover these fillets with ½ the butter mixture, and sprinkle with lemon pepper.
Cover those fillets with foil and bake for 15 minutes.
Serve warm with the rest of the butter mixture on top.

Per serving: Calories: 272; Carbs: 3.38 g; Protein: 22.04 g; Total Fat: 19.07 g; Fiber: 0.5 g; Sugar: 1.2 g; Sodium: 426 mg; Potassium: 421 mg; Calcium (Ca): 28 mg; Vitamin B-12: 2.79 µg; Vitamin D: 41 IU

Fish Soup

Prep Time: 10 minutes | **Cook Time:** 30 minutes | **Servings**: 5

Ingredients:
½ onion, chopped
1 clove garlic, minced
1 tablespoon chili powder
1 ½ cups chicken broth
1 teaspoon ground cumin
½ cup chopped green bell pepper
½ cup shrimp
½ pound cod fillets
¾ cup plain yogurt

Directions:
Spray a large saucepan with the cooking spray.
Add the onions and sauté them for 5 minutes over medium-high heat.
Add the garlic and chili powder and sauté for 2 minutes longer.
Add the chicken broth and cumin, stir well; bring to a boil and then adjust the heat to low.
Cover the pan and cook the food for 20 minutes.
When the time is up, add the shrimp, green bell pepper and cod, increase the heat and bring to a boil again, then lower the heat, cover the pan and wait for 5 minutes.
Slowly stir in the yogurt and heat for another minute.
Serve and enjoy.

Per serving: Calories: 84; Carbs: 4.67 g; Protein: 11.83 g; Total Fat: 2.06 g; Fiber: 0.9 g; Sugar: 2.86 g; Sodium: 590 mg; Potassium: 260 mg; Calcium (Ca): 83 mg; Vitamin B-12: 1.14 µg; Vitamin D: 10 IU

Chili Mussels with Parsley

Prep Time: 7 minutes | **Cook Time:** 10 minutes | **Servings**: 4

Ingredients:
1-pound mussels
1 chili pepper, chopped
1 cup chicken stock
½ cup milk
1 teaspoon olive oil
1 teaspoon minced garlic
1 teaspoon ground coriander
½ teaspoon salt
1 cup fresh parsley, chopped
4 tablespoons lemon juice

Directions:
In the saucepan, add the milk, chili pepper, chicken stock, olive oil, minced garlic, ground coriander, salt and lemon juice.
Bring the liquid to a boil and then add mussels.
Boil the mussel for 4 minutes or until they will open the shells.
Add chopped parsley and mix up the meal well.
Remove it from the heat, serve and enjoy.

Per serving: Calories: 136; Carbs: 9.28 g; Protein: 15.7 g; Total Fat: 4 g; Fiber: 0.7 g; Sugar: 2.92 g; Sodium: 868 mg; Potassium: 562 mg; Calcium (Ca): 94 mg; Vitamin B-12: 13.77 µg; Vitamin D: 14 IU

Fried Scallops in Cream

Prep Time: 10 minutes | **Cook Time:** 10 minutes | **Servings**: 4

Ingredients:
½ cup heavy cream
1 teaspoon fresh rosemary
½ teaspoon dried cumin
½ teaspoon garlic, diced
8 oz. bay scallops
1 teaspoon olive oil
½ teaspoon salt
¼ teaspoon chili flakes

Directions:
Sprinkle the scallops with salt, chili flakes and dried cumin.
In the skillet, heat the olive oil until hot; add the scallops, fresh rosemary, dice garlic and then roast the scallops for 2 minutes on each side.
Add heavy cream and bring the prepared mixture to a boil. Boil the food for almost 1 minute.
When done, serve and enjoy.

Per serving: Calories: 103; Carbs: 2.58 g; Protein: 7.25 g; Total Fat: 7.05 g; Fiber: 0.1 g; Sugar: 0.44 g; Sodium: 524 mg; Potassium: 138 mg; Calcium (Ca): 18 mg; Vitamin B-12: 0.83 µg; Vitamin D: 5 IU

Tuna Mushroom Casserole

Prep Time: 10 minutes | **Cook Time:** 40 minutes | **Servings**: 3

Ingredients:
2 cups macaroni
2 (5 ounce) cans tuna, drained
1 (10 ounce) can mushrooms, drained
1 cup water
1 ⅓ cups soy milk
¼ teaspoon black pepper
1 cup dry white bread crumbs
3 tablespoons melted butter
2 teaspoons dried thyme, crushed

Directions:
In a mixing bowl, mix up the butter, bread crumbs and thyme.
Mix tuna and other recipe ingredients in a baking dish.
Drizzle this crumbs mixture over the top of the tuna mixture.
Bake this casserole in the oven for 40 minutes or until golden brown.
Serve.

Per serving: Calories: 340; Carbs: 36.6 g; Protein: 17.26 g; Total Fat: 15.06 g; Fiber: 3.1 g; Sugar: 7.27 g; Sodium: 455 mg; Potassium: 331 mg; Calcium (Ca): 142 mg; Vitamin B-12: 1.23 µg; Vitamin D: 77 IU

Poached Halibut

Prep Time: 10 minutes | **Cook Time:** 10 minutes | **Servings**: 4

Ingredients:
1-pound halibut
⅓ cup butter
1 rosemary sprig
½ teaspoon ground black pepper
1 teaspoon salt
1 teaspoon honey
¼ cup of orange juice
1 teaspoon cornstarch

Directions:
Sprinkle the halibut with salt and ground black pepper.
In the saucepan, melt the butter over medium heat; add the rosemary sprig, halibut and poach them for 4 minutes.
In the skillet, pour orange juice, add the honey and bring the liquid to a boil.
Add cornstarch and whisk until the liquid starts to be thick, then remove it from the heat.
Transfer the poached halibut to the plate and cut it on
Place every fish serving on the serving plate and top with orange sauce.

Per serving: Calories: 364; Carbs: 4.51 g; Protein: 16.69 g; Total Fat: 30.94 g; Fiber: 0.2 g; Sugar: 3.05 g; Sodium: 793 mg; Potassium: 359 mg; Calcium (Ca): 12 mg; Vitamin B-12: 1.17 µg; Vitamin D: 1255 IU

Italian Sea Bass

Prep Time: 12 -15 minutes | **Cook Time:** 7 minutes | **Serves:** 1

Ingredients:
5 oz. sea bass fillet, skinless, boneless
1 teaspoon Italian seasoning
1 teaspoon sweet paprika
¼ teaspoon salt
¼ teaspoon black pepper
1 teaspoon olive oil

Directions:
Preheat the skillet with the oil until hot.
Put the sea bass and the rest of the ingredients in the hot skillet and cook it for 4 minutes. Then flip the fish on another side and cook it for 3 minutes more.

Per serving: Calories: 195; Carbs: 3.37 g; Protein: 26.66 g; Total Fat: 7.66 g; Fiber: 1.4 g; Sugar: 0.56 g; Sodium: 888 mg; Potassium: 454 mg; Calcium (Ca): 23 mg; Vitamin B-12: 0.43 µg; Vitamin D: 320 IU

Shrimp with Snow Peas

Prep Time: 20 minutes | **Cook Time:** 12 minutes | **Servings**: 4

Ingredients:
2 tablespoons of extra-virgin olive oil
1 tablespoon of minced peeled fresh ginger
2 cups of snow peas
1½ cups of frozen baby peas
3 tablespoons of water
1-pound shrimp, shelled and deveined
2 tablespoons of low-sodium soy sauce
⅛ teaspoon of black pepper

Directions:
In a large wok, heat the olive oil over medium heat; add the ginger and sauté for 1 to 2 minutes until fragrant; add the snow peas and sauté for 2 to 3 minutes until they are tender-crisp; add the baby peas, water and stir.
Cover the wok and steam the food for 2 to 3 minutes, or until the vegetables are tender; stir in the shrimp and stir-fry for almost 3 to 4 minutes, or until the shrimp have curled and turned pink.
Add the soy sauce and pepper; stir well. Serve and enjoy.

Per serving: Calories: 211; Carbs: 16.32 g; Protein: 28.22 g; Total Fat: 3.89 g; Fiber: 3.8 g; Sugar: 0.13 g; Sodium: 483 mg; Potassium: 616 mg; Calcium (Ca): 99 mg; Vitamin B-12: 0.01 µg; Vitamin D: 0 IU

Lemon Rosemary Salmon

Prep Time: 15 minutes | **Cook Time:** 35 minutes | **Servings**: 3

Ingredients:
¼ cup butter, melted
¼ cup white wine
1 lemon, juiced
5 cloves garlic, chopped
1 bunch fresh rosemary, stems trimmed
1 (1 pound) salmon fillet

Directions:
At 375 degrees F, preheat your oven.
In the baking pan, mix up all the ingredients.
Bake the food for 25 minutes.
Serve.

Per serving: Calories: 330; Carbs: 3.1 g; Protein: 31.1 g; Total Fat: 21.15 g; Fiber: 0.2 g; Sugar: 0.68 g; Sodium: 80 mg; Potassium: 711 mg; Calcium (Ca): 35 mg; Vitamin B-12: 4.57 µg; Vitamin D: 383 IU

Lemon-Pepper Salmon

Prep Time: 10 minutes | **Cook Time:** 20 minutes | **Servings**: 5

Ingredients:
2 tablespoons olive oil
4 (4 ounce) salmon steaks
1 teaspoon minced garlic
1 tablespoon lemon pepper
2-¼ cups water
1 cup chopped fresh cilantro
1 cup uncooked couscous

Directions:
In the skillet, heat the olive oil over medium heat; add the salmon steaks, garlic, lemon pepper, cilantro and ¼ cup of water, cook the food for 15 minutes or until the salmon steaks are easily flaked with a fork.
In the pot, bring 2 cups of water to boil. Remove the pot from heat and mix in couscous.
Cover and let sit for 5 minutes.
Serve the cooked salmon over couscous and drizzle with sauce from skillet.

Per serving: Calories: 120; Carbs: 8.45 g; Protein: 6.31 g; Total Fat: 6.76 g; Fiber: 0.7 g; Sugar: 0.52 g; Sodium: 30 mg; Potassium: 146 mg; Calcium (Ca): 15 mg; Vitamin B-12: 1.35 µg; Vitamin D: 100 IU

Salsa Shrimp

Prep Time: 12 -15 minutes | **Cook Time:** 14 minutes | **Serves:** 2

Ingredients:
1-pound shrimps, peeled
1 tablespoon orange juice
½ jalapeno, diced
1 tablespoon salsa Verde
¼ teaspoon all spices
⅛ teaspoon cayenne pepper
1 tablespoon olive oil
¼ teaspoon salt

Directions:
Heat a suitable pan with the oil over medium heat, add the shrimp, orange juice, and the rest of the ingredients.
Toss and roast them for 6 minutes.
Then flip them on another side and roast for 8 minutes more.

Per serving: Calories: 261; Carbs: 1.93 g; Protein: 45.83 g; Total Fat: 7.99 g; Fiber: 0.3 g; Sugar: 1.17 g; Sodium: 625 mg; Potassium: 650 mg; Calcium (Ca): 151 mg; Vitamin B-12: 0 µg; Vitamin D: 0 IU

Turmeric Tuna Steaks

Prep Time: 5-7 minutes | **Cook Time:** 25 minutes | **Serves:** 3

Ingredients:
14 oz. tuna steaks
1 teaspoon sweet paprika
2 tablespoons olive oil
1 teaspoon turmeric powder
½ teaspoon fresh ginger, minced
1 teaspoon lemon juice
¼ teaspoon ground black pepper

Directions:
At 360 degrees F, preheat your oven.
In a roasting pan, mix the tuna steaks with the paprika and the rest of the ingredients.
Bake at 380 degrees F for 25 minutes and serve.

Per serving: Calories: 231; Carbs: 1.62 g; Protein: 32.57 g; Total Fat: 9.79 g; Fiber: 0.6 g; Sugar: 0.35 g; Sodium: 61 mg; Potassium: 638 mg; Calcium (Ca): 10 mg; Vitamin B-12: 2.75 µg; Vitamin D: 91 IU

Salmon with Almonds

Prep Time: 9 minutes | **Cook Time:** 12 minutes | **Serves:** 3

Ingredients:
2-pound salmon fillets
¼ cup lemon juice
2 tablespoons almonds, chopped
1 tablespoon olive oil
1 teaspoon ground black pepper
1 teaspoon salt
1 teaspoon lemon zest, grated
½ teaspoon Italian seasoning

Directions:
Heat a suitable pan with the oil over medium heat.
Add the salmon and the rest of the ingredients.
Cook the mix for 6 minutes on each side.
Serve with a salad.

Per serving: Calories: 416; Carbs: 2.58 g; Protein: 61.27 g; Total Fat: 16.38 g; Fiber: 0.5 g; Sugar: 0.65 g; Sodium: 960 mg; Potassium: 1344 mg; Calcium (Ca): 42 mg; Vitamin B-12: 9.07 µg; Vitamin D: 742 IU

Limey Scallops

Prep Time: 9 minutes | **Cook Time:** 10 minutes | **Serves:** 2

Ingredients:
1 tablespoon olive oil
1 tablespoon lemon juice
5 garlic cloves, diced
1 teaspoon lime juice
¼ teaspoon cayenne pepper
12 oz. scallops

Directions:
Put the oil in the skillet and heat up.
Add diced garlic and roast it for 2 minutes.
Then add the scallops and the rest of the ingredients.
Roast the scallops for 4 minutes from each side on medium-low heat and serve.

Per serving: Calories: 191; Carbs: 8.77 g; Protein: 21.06 g; Total Fat: 7.68 g; Fiber: 0.3 g; Sugar: 0.34 g; Sodium: 668 mg; Potassium: 395 mg; Calcium (Ca): 25 mg; Vitamin B-12: 2.4 µg; Vitamin D: 2 IU

Roasted Cod with Capers

Prep Time: 9 minutes | **Cook Time:** 15 minutes | **Serves:** 4

Ingredients:
2-pound cod fillets, boneless
1 teaspoon sweet paprika
1 teaspoon white pepper
1 teaspoon chili flakes
2 tablespoons chives, chopped
1 tablespoon capers
1 teaspoon olive oil

Directions:
In a baking pan, mix the cod with paprika and the rest of the ingredients.
Transfer the skillet with fish in the oven and cook it for 15 minutes at 365 degrees F.

Per serving: Calories: 173; Carbs: 1.23 g; Protein: 34.97 g; Total Fat: 2.27 g; Fiber: 0.7 g; Sugar: 0.14 g; Sodium: 758 mg; Potassium: 565 mg; Calcium (Ca): 26 mg; Vitamin B-12: 4.49 µg; Vitamin D: 45 IU

Shrimps Skewers

Prep Time: 26 minutes | **Cook Time:** 10 minutes | **Serves:** 4

Ingredients:
14 oz. shrimps, peeled and deveined
1 tablespoon lemon juice
1 teaspoon chili powder
2 tablespoons olive oil
1 teaspoon dried cilantro
½ teaspoon salt

Directions:
In the mixing bowl, mix up the shrimp with the rest of the ingredients and toss.
Then string the shrimp on the skewers and put in the preheated grill.
Cook the meal at 375 degrees F for 5 minutes from each side.

Per serving: Calories: 147; Carbs: 0.6 g; Protein: 20.05 g; Total Fat: 7.36 g; Fiber: 0.2 g; Sugar: 0.15 g; Sodium: 428 mg; Potassium: 280 mg; Calcium (Ca): 66 mg; Vitamin B-12: 0 µg; Vitamin D: 0 IU

Chapter 5 Vegetarian Recipes

Tasty Cabbage Stew

Prep Time: 20 minutes | **Cook Time:** 40 minutes | **Serves:** 12

Ingredients:
1 head cabbage, diced
¼ cup canola oil
1 onion, diced
2 teaspoons minced garlic
4 Roma (plum) tomatoes, diced
1 cup water
6-ounce tomato paste
1 pinch red pepper flake
1 pinch seasoned salt

Directions:
In a pot, add cabbage, pour in salted water, and bring together to a boil.
Simmer over medium-low heat for 10 minutes. Then drain.
In a saucepan, heat canola oil over medium heat.
When the canola oil is heated, add garlic and onion and cook for 5 to 7 minutes.
Add tomatoes to the garlic mixture and then transfer together to the saucepan. Cook for 10 to 15 minutes.
When cooked, transfer to a serving plate.
Serve and enjoy!

Per serving: Calories: 70; Carbs: 6.89 g; Protein: 1.41 g; Total Fat: 4.75 g; Fiber: 1.8 g; Sugar: 3.47 g; Sodium: 35 mg; Potassium: 270 mg; Calcium (Ca): 32 mg; Vitamin B-12: 0 µg; Vitamin D: 0 IU

Baked Cheese and Potato with Olives

Prep Time: 15 minutes | **Cook Time:** 40 minutes | **Serves:** 1

Ingredients:
¼ teaspoon onion powder
1 medium russet potato, scrubbed and peeled
1 tablespoon chives, chopped
1 tablespoon Kalamata olives
1 teaspoon olive oil
⅛ teaspoon salt
a dollop of vegan butter
a dollop of vegan cream cheese

Directions:
Heat your air fryer to 400 degrees F.
Cook the potato in your air fryer for about 40 minutes, flipping once halfway cooking.
In a mixing bowl, mix together the potatoes, olive oil, onion powder, vegan butter, and salt.
Add the vegan cream cheese, chives, Kalamata olives, and other vegan topping as you like to serve. Enjoy!

Per serving: Calories: 354; Carbs: 67.84 g; Protein: 8.21 g; Total Fat: 6.82 g; Fiber: 5.2 g; Sugar: 2.42 g; Sodium: 395 mg; Potassium: 1556 mg; Calcium (Ca): 62 mg; Vitamin B-12: 0.01 µg; Vitamin D: 1 IU

Coconut Eggplant Curry

Prep Time: 15 minutes | **Cook Time:** 30 minutes | **Serves:** 2

Ingredients:
½ tablespoon pepper
½ cup coconut milk
1 tin tomatoes, chopped roughly
1 tablespoon ground coriander
1 tablespoon turmeric
1 tablespoon gram masala powder or curry powder
1 clove garlic
1 red onion
1 tablespoon olive oil
½ tablespoon salt
1 aborigine (medium)
Optional:
1-2 tablespoons sugar or mango chutney

Directions:
Cook the rice according to the packet directions. Cut the aubergine into tiny cubes.
In a wide pan, add olive oil and fry the aubergine cubes over high heat for 3 to 4 minutes, stirring occasionally to avoid smoke.
Add the chopped onion in the pan and cook over medium heat for 5 to 6 minutes.
Mix in the diced garlic, curry powder, ground cilantro, and turmeric, stir and cook for 3 to 4 minutes.
Then add the tomato slices and coconut milk.
Season with salt and roughly boil for 15 minutes, or until the coconut milk gets thicker to reach your desired consistency.
Add a little sweeter, like honey or mango chutney, as you like. Serve with salt and pepper as you like.

Per serving: Calories: 269; Carbs: 19.86 g; Protein: 3.38 g; Total Fat: 21.49 g; Fiber: 4.5 g; Sugar: 10.62 g; Sodium: 1761 mg; Potassium: 535 mg; Calcium (Ca): 45 mg; Vitamin B-12: 0 µg; Vitamin D: 0 IU

Baked Eggs with Spinach

Prep Time: 10 minutes | **Cook Time:** 9 minutes | **Serves:** 6

Ingredients:
2 cups fresh spinach, chopped
12 large eggs
½ cup heavy cream
¾ cup low-sodium parmesan cheese, shredded
Salt and ground black pepper, as required

Directions:
Heat your oven to 425 degrees F before cooking.
Prepare a 12-cup muffin tin and grease.
Divide spinach in each muffin cup and crack an egg over spinach. Drizzle heavy cream over the egg and bake for 7 to 9 minutes, or until the eggs reach your desired doneness.
Serve and enjoy!

Per serving: Calories: 237; Carbs: 2.07 g; Protein: 18.29 g; Total Fat: 17.01 g; Fiber: 0.3 g; Sugar: 0.8 g; Sodium: 162 mg; Potassium: 220 mg; Calcium (Ca): 174 mg; Vitamin B-12: 1.08 µg; Vitamin D: 87 IU

Zucchini Sushi Rolls

Prep Time: 10 minutes | **Cook Time:** 0 minutes | **Serves:** 4

Ingredients:
1 cup cooked quinoa
2 small-medium zucchini
1 carrot cut into strips
1 avocado, cut into strips
A bunch of fresh mint leaves chopped
Light soya sauce to serve
Wasabi to serve

Directions:
Cover with cling film a bamboo sheet. In the meantime, cut the zucchini lengthwise into very thin strips with the help of a peeler.
Arrange the thin zucchini slices slightly overlapping each other, carrying on until you have a long strip enough to make 4 rolls out of it.
Consider a couple of extra cm per side, as the edges will be chopped off to ensure all rolls are even.
Place ½ cup quinoa on top, press a thin layer of quinoa onto the bottom. Make sure you have a even layer that covers horizontally half the zucchini bed.
Arrange carrots and avocado into a long even strip on top of quinoa.
Start to roll up, making sure to keep the roll tight, and gently pressing down with your fingers all the way until you reach the end. Be careful not to squeeze out the roll filling.
Once the roll is ready, you can cover in cling film and refrigerate for 15 minutes to firm it up.
Or you can use a sharp knife and carefully cut it into 4 even rolls, chopping the two ends off.
Serve accompanied by soy sauce and wasabi, or refrigerate for up to 3 hours and serve later.

Per serving: Calories: 138; Carbs: 14.51 g; Protein: 3.24 g; Total Fat: 8.29 g; Fiber: 4.8 g; Sugar: 0.84 g; Sodium: 17 mg; Potassium: 358 mg; Calcium (Ca): 17 mg; Vitamin B-12: 0 µg; Vitamin D: 0 IU

Cheddar Broccoli Waffles

Prep Time: 10 minutes | **Cook Time:** 8 minutes | **Serves:** 2

Ingredients:
⅓ cup broccoli, finely chopped
¼ cup low-fat cheddar cheese, shredded
1 egg
½ teaspoon garlic powder
½ teaspoon dried onion, minced
Salt and ground black pepper, as required

Directions:
Prepare a mini waffle iron. Heat in advance and then grease it.
Mix together all the ingredients in a medium bowl until well combined.
Add half the mixture to the prepared mini muffin iron and cook until golden brown about 3 to 4 minutes.
Repeat with the remaining mixture.
Serve and enjoy!

Per serving: Calories: 147; Carbs: 8.03 g; Protein: 8.54 g; Total Fat: 5.8 g; Fiber: 1.3 g; Sugar: 4.38 g; Sodium: 170 mg; Potassium: 180 mg; Calcium (Ca): 158 mg; Vitamin B-12: 0.33 µg; Vitamin D: 21 IU

Mexican Baked Zucchini

Prep Time: 10 minutes | **Cook Time:** 30 minutes | **Serves:** 4

Ingredients:
1 tablespoon olive oil
1-½ pounds' zucchini, cubed
½ cup chopped onion
½ teaspoon garlic salt
½ teaspoon paprika
½ teaspoon dried oregano
½ teaspoon pepper, or to taste
½ cup cooked long-grain rice
½ cup cooked pinto beans
1-¼ cups salsa
¾ cup low-fat shredded Cheddar cheese

Directions:
Prepare a baking pan and grease with olive oil.
Then add onions and zucchini and cook at 360 degrees F for 10 minutes.
Add oregano, paprika, garlic salt, and cayenne and mix well to season.
Add beans, rice, and salsa, stir, and cook for 5 minutes.
Mix in cheddar cheese and use foil to cover the pan.
Cook at 390 degrees F until bubbly, about 15 minutes.
When cooked, transfer to a serving plate.
Serve and enjoy!

Per serving: Calories: 204; Carbs: 19.01 g; Protein: 12.82 g; Total Fat: 9.56 g; Fiber: 4.5 g; Sugar: 2.85 g; Sodium: 487 mg; Potassium: 681 mg; Calcium (Ca): 225 mg; Vitamin B-12: 0.21 µg; Vitamin D: 4 IU

Baked Eggs in Avocado Halves

Prep Time: 10 minutes | **Cook Time:** 15 minutes | **Serves:** 2

Ingredients:
1 avocado, halved and pitted
2 eggs
Salt and ground black pepper, as required
¼ cup cherry tomatoes, halved
2 cups fresh baby spinach

Directions:
Heat your oven to 425 degrees F before cooking.
Scoop off about 2 tablespoons of flesh from avocado halves.
Arrange the avocado halves on a small baking dish and crack an egg inside each avocado halves. Sprinkle salt and black pepper to season and bake until the eggs reach your desired doneness, about 15 minutes.
When cooked, transfer to serving plates and add the cherry tomatoes and spinach alongside to serve.

Per serving: Calories: 240; Carbs: 12.28 g; Protein: 8.86 g; Total Fat: 19.08 g; Fiber: 7.8 g; Sugar: 2.23 g; Sodium: 95 mg; Potassium: 794 mg; Calcium (Ca): 71 mg; Vitamin B-12: 0.39 µg; Vitamin D: 36 IU

Stuffed Banana Pepper

Prep Time: 5 minutes | **Cook Time:** 10 minutes | **Serves:** 8

Ingredients:
½ teaspoon red chili powder
½ teaspoon turmeric powder
1 onion, chopped
1 package firm tofu, crumbled
1 teaspoon coriander powder
3 tablespoons coconut oil
8 banana peppers, top end sliced and seeded
Salt to taste

Directions:
Heat your air fryer for 5 minutes before cooking.
Combine onion, tofu, coconut oil, red chili powder, coriander powder, salt, and turmeric powder in a mixing bowl and mix well.
Fill the banana peppers with the tofu mixture.
Cook the stuffed banana peppers in the preheated air fryer at 325 degrees F for 10 minutes.
When cooked, transfer to a serving plate.
Serve and enjoy!

Per serving: Calories: 127; Carbs: 7.48 g; Protein: 7.48 g; Total Fat: 8.77 g; Fiber: 1.9 g; Sugar: 2.9 g; Sodium: 34 mg; Potassium: 277 mg; Calcium (Ca): 389 mg; Vitamin B-12: 0 µg; Vitamin D: 0 IU

Creamy Spinach Waffles

Prep Time: 10 minutes | **Cook Time:** 20 minutes | **Serves:** 4

Ingredients:
1 large egg, beaten
1 cup ricotta cheese, crumbled
½ cup part-skim mozzarella cheese, shredded
¼ cup low-sodium Parmesan cheese, grated
4 ounces frozen spinach, thawed
1 garlic clove, minced
Salt and ground black pepper, as required

Directions:
Prepare a mini waffle iron. Heat and then grease.
Stir together all the ingredient in a medium bowl until well combined.
Add ¼ of the mixture to the prepared waffle iron and cook until golden brown, about 4 to 5 minutes.
Repeat with the rest mixture.
Serve and enjoy!

Per serving: Calories: 188; Carbs: 7.61 g; Protein: 16.06 g; Total Fat: 10.61 g; Fiber: 1 g; Sugar: 1.15 g; Sodium: 136 mg; Potassium: 280 mg; Calcium (Ca): 350 mg; Vitamin B-12: 0.47 µg; Vitamin D: 17 IU

Guacamole Deviled Eggs

Prep Time: 5 minutes | **Cook Time:** 11 minutes | **Serves:** 3

Ingredients:
6 large eggs
2 medium avocados
1 teaspoon chopped chipotle
½ red onion chopped
¼ cup chopped cilantro;
2 tablespoons fresh lemon juice;
Salt and pepper

Directions:
In a pot of boiling water, fold in the eggs and allow to cook for almost 11 minutes.
In the meantime, prepare the guacamole. Cut the avocado in half and scoop out the flesh.
Put avocados and the remaining ingredients into a blender and mix until creamy, taste to season with salt and pepper.
Pour the guacamole into a piping bag and refrigerate until ready to use.
When the eggs are ready, cool them under cold running water, and peel them.
Cut each egg horizontally in half and scoop out the cooked yolks. You can use them for another recipe or in salads.
Pipe the guacamole into each egg half, taste to season and serve.

Per serving: Calories: 368; Carbs: 14.74 g; Protein: 15.51 g; Total Fat: 29.31 g; Fiber: 9.4 g; Sugar: 2.41 g; Sodium: 166 mg; Potassium: 833 mg; Calcium (Ca): 78 mg; Vitamin B-12: 0.89 µg; Vitamin D: 82 IU

Vegan Pesto

Prep Time: 10 minutes | **Cook Time:** 0 minutes | **Serves:** 12

Ingredients:
2 garlic cloves
2 tablespoons nutritional yeast
2 cups fresh basil leaves
⅔ cup raw macadamia nuts
3 tablespoons olive oil
3-4 tablespoons water
Sea salt and ground black pepper, to taste

Directions:
Add basil leaves, macadamia, garlic, and nutritional yeast in a cup a food processor or blender and blend until a thick paste forms, scrapping sides.
Add extra virgin olive oil and water, one tablespoon at a time, until smooth.
Add sea salt and ground black pepper to time.
Enjoy!

Per serving: Calories: 90; Carbs: 1.94 g; Protein: 1.36 g; Total Fat: 9.08 g; Fiber: 0.9 g; Sugar: 0.4 g; Sodium: 90 mg; Potassium: 95 mg; Calcium (Ca): 11 mg; Vitamin B-12: 0.02 µg; Vitamin D: 0 IU

Cauldron Chicken Curry

Prep Time: 10 minutes | **Cook Time:** 20 minutes | **Serves:** 6

Ingredients:
Curry paste:
1 tablespoon whole coriander seeds
2 teaspoons whole cumin seeds
1 teaspoon whole black peppercorns
1 teaspoon coarse salt
3 serrano chilies
½ cup fresh cilantro
2 stalk fresh lemongrass
8 garlic clove
2 scallions
2 tablespoons chopped peeled fresh ginger
2 tablespoons fresh lime juice
1 tablespoon grated lime zest

Stew:
2-ounce spinach
1 can unsweetened regular almond milk
1 can unsweetened light almond milk
1 medium zucchini
12-ounce boneless, skinless chicken breasts
12-ounce boneless, skinless chicken thighs
Coarse salt and ground pepper
¾ cup fresh basil
Serrano chilies
Squeamish squash with rice
Lime wedges

Directions:
Make the curry paste: grind coriander seeds, cumin seeds, peppercorns, and salt with a mortar and pestle, or with the bottom of a heavy skillet.
Add remaining ingredients, and grind until a paste forms.
Make the stew: puree 5 tablespoons curry paste, the spinach, and 1 cup regular almond milk in a blender until smooth.
Reserve remaining curry paste for another use.
Bring remaining regular almond milk and the light almond milk to a boil in a medium dutch oven or heavy stockpot.
Reduce heat, stir in curry-spinach mixture, and simmer for 5 minutes.
Add zucchini, and cook until slightly tender, about 5 minutes.
Add chicken, and season with salt and pepper. Cook until zucchini is tender and chicken is cooked through, about 5 minutes.
Add basil, and garnish with serrano chiles.
Serve with squeamish squash with rice and lime wedges.

Per serving: Calories: 265; Carbs: 11.55 g; Protein: 35.04 g; Total Fat: 9.74 g; Fiber: 1.2 g; Sugar: 5.29 g; Sodium: 820 mg; Potassium: 747 mg; Calcium (Ca): 189 mg; Vitamin B-12: 0.82 µg; Vitamin D: 39 IU

Pumpkin and Kale with Polenta

Prep Time: 10 minutes | **Cook Time:** 20 minutes | **Serves:** 4

Ingredients:
Pumpkin and Kale with Creamy Polenta:
1½ cups polenta
4½ cups water
½ cup grated parmesan
½ small pumpkin
1 small red chili pepper
4 sprigs fresh thyme
Vegetable oil
1 garlic clove chopped
7-ounce curly kale chopped, veins removed
⅓ leek, sliced
Black pepper
Salt
4-ounce mozzarella
For the Dressing:
5 tablespoons olive oil
2 teaspoons balsamic vinegar
1 teaspoon lemon juice
1 teaspoon demerara sugar
2 tablespoons chopped basil
Black pepper
Salt
4 tablespoons pomegranate seeds to serve

Directions:
In a pot, bring water with a tablespoon of salt to a boil. Gradually add polenta, cover with a lid and reduce the heat to low. Cook for almost 10 minutes, stirring frequently. Remove from the heat, add parmesan, cover and let rest for 15 minutes.
Meanwhile, slice the pumpkin. Heat a lug of vegetable oil in a large pan or wok over medium high heat. Stir in pumpkin and cook for about 8 minutes. Chop red chili pepper and thyme leaves and add them before the pumpkin is ready. Transfer to a plate and put the pan or wok back on the stove.
Add a bit of oil to the pan and once it's hot, add garlic and kale. Add salt and black pepper to taste then cook until soft, about 4 minutes. Transfer to a plate.
Add leek slices and cook until soft and slightly golden, about 4 minutes.
Make the dressing: combine olive oil, balsamic vinegar, lemon juice, demerara sugar, chopped basil, a pinch of salt and black pepper.
Arrange polenta, pumpkin, kale and leek on two plates. Add sliced mozzarella.
Serve with balsamic dressing and pomegranate seeds. Enjoy!

Per serving: Calories: 368; Carbs: 32.48 g; Protein: 17.59 g; Total Fat: 19.61 g; Fiber: 4 g; Sugar: 4.68 g; Sodium: 720 mg; Potassium: 488 mg; Calcium (Ca): 479 mg; Vitamin B-12: 0.37 µg; Vitamin D: 0 IU

Coleslaw with Barberries

Prep Time: 10 minutes | **Cook Time:** 0 minutes | **Serves:** 4

Ingredients:
1 lb. mixed cabbage
A few Brussels sprouts, shredded
1 medium carrot, peeled and grated
1 small parsnip, peeled and grated
¼ small celeriac, peeled and grated
1 small beetroot, peeled and grated
1 small red onion, peeled and sliced
Handful of parsley, large stalks removed
Handful of mint leaves
Handful of dried barberries, soaked, drained and rinsed
Handful of sunflower seeds, toasted
Handful of pumpkin seeds, toasted

Dressing
2-3 tablespoons olive oil
1 lemon or lime
Sea salt

Directions:
Shred both the cabbages and Brussels sprouts by hand or using the slicer attachment of a food processor and place into a suitable mixing bowl.
Stir in the parsnip, grated carrot, celeriac and beetroot.
Slice the red onion and place into a small bowl of cold water, making sure it is fully submerged. This will help to remove the strong pungency of the onion flavor, and crisp up the texture.
Chop the fresh herbs roughly, and add to the grated vegetables.
To make the dressing, add lime juice with the olive oil and red chilli. Time and add enough agave syrup to slightly sweeten.
Drain the onion in a sieve, then add to the other vegetables.
Pour over the dressing and mix the coleslaw thoroughly.
Season with a pinch of salt and taste. Add a little more salt, oil or lemon if necessary.
Sprinkle over the sunflower, barberries, and pumpkin seeds.
This coleslaw will keep for up to 3 days in a container in the fridge.

Per serving: Calories: 168; Carbs: 16.77 g; Protein: 4 g; Total Fat: 10.9 g; Fiber: 4.7 g; Sugar: 8.27 g; Sodium: 100 mg; Potassium: 564 mg; Calcium (Ca): 88 mg; Vitamin B-12: 0 µg; Vitamin D: 0 IU

Balsamic Arugula Lentil Salad

Prep Time: 5 minutes | **Cook Time:** 7 minutes | **Serves:** 2

Ingredients:
1-2 tablespoons balsamic vinegar
¾ cup cashews
1 handful arugula / rocket
1 cup brown lentils, cooked
whole wheat bread slices
5-6 sun-dried tomatoes in oil
1 chili / jalapeño
1 tablespoon olive oil
1 onion
salt and pepper to taste

Optional:
1 tablespoon honey
1 small handful of raisins

Directions:
In a pan, toast the cashews over low heat for about 3 to 4 minutes.
Add the toasted cashews into a pot of salad.
Heat ⅓ of the olive oil over low heat in the pan. Add the diced onion and fry for 3 minutes.
Meanwhile, cut the chili/ jalapeno and sun-dried tomatoes. Then add to the pan and fry about 1 to 2 minutes.
Slice the bread into large croutons. Transfer the cooked onion mixture into a large container.
Add the remaining oil in the pan and cook the large croutons until crispy.
Add salt and pepper to season.
Add the rinsed arugula in the bowl and add the lentils. Blend all together.
Season with salt, pepper, and balsamic vinegar.
Top with the croutons.
Serve and enjoy!

Per serving: Calories: 506; Carbs: 45.36 g; Protein: 16.97 g; Total Fat: 32.5 g; Fiber: 5.4 g; Sugar: 10.68 g; Sodium: 93 mg; Potassium: 864 mg; Calcium (Ca): 59 mg; Vitamin B-12: 0 µg; Vitamin D: 0 IU

Cashew Leek Soup with Potato

Prep Time: 5 minutes | **Cook Time:** 25 minutes | **Serves:** 4

Ingredients:
4 medium-sized leeks
1 large potato
1 ½ cups vegetable stock
½ cup (75 grams) raw cashews soaked overnight
½ cup (120 ml) water
1 head of garlic
⅛ teaspoon olive oil
½ teaspoon lemon juice
½ teaspoon salt
Seeds of ½ a pomegranate
A few herb leaves - basil, mint, cilantro, chives, etc.

Directions:
In a saucepan, add a couple tablespoons of water and bring to a boil over medium heat.
Slice separately the white part and light green part of the leeks. The more green parts you add, the more off-white the soup will be.
Add the leeks in the pan and let it sweat for 5 minutes.
Peel the potatoes and dice. Then add to the pan and let it sweat for about couple of minutes.
Pour 1 cup of vegetable stock, cover the pan partially, and cook until the vegetables are very soft and failing apart, about 20 minutes.
Cut off the top of the head of garlic and drizzle over ⅛ teaspoon of oil.
Roast in the microwave on high until soft, about 2 minutes.
Drain the cashews and blend together with ½ cup of fresh water until creamy.
Mix together the cooked mixture with as much of the roasted garlics as you like.
Season with lemon juice and salt as you desired. Blend until creamy.
Add vegetable stock as you like.
Add the herbs and pomegranate seeds to garnish.
Serve hot or cold!

Per serving: Calories: 181; Carbs: 22.95 g; Protein: 5.57 g; Total Fat: 8.4 g; Fiber: 2.7 g; Sugar: 1.89 g; Sodium: 301 mg; Potassium: 529 mg; Calcium (Ca): 28 mg; Vitamin B-12: 0 µg; Vitamin D: 0 IU

Vegan Pad Thai

Prep Time: 15 minutes | **Cook Time:** 15 minutes | **Serves:** 4

Ingredients:
7-ounce rice noodles
1 garlic clove, minced
1 red chili, sliced
6 tablespoons snow peas
100 g sprouting broccoli
4 baby corns chopped
5 tablespoons red cabbage, chopped
1 large carrot, peeled and julienned
1.7-ounce dry roasted peanuts, chopped
Juice of 1 lime
2 spring onions, chopped
Handful of fresh cilantro leaves, chopped

For the Sauce:
2-ounce gluten-free soy sauce or tamari or fish sauce for non vegan version
1 tablespoon tamarind paste, thinned with 2 teaspoon of water
2 tablespoons brown sugar
A pinch of red pepper flakes

Directions:
Soak the noodles in lukewarm water for 6-7 minutes. Then drain and rinse under cool water and set aside in a colander.
In a small bowl, combine together soy sauce, tamarind, sugar, and red pepper flakes.
Heat a large wok over medium heat. Swirl a glug of olive oil in the pan, add in garlic and chilli and stir fry for a few seconds. Remove them from the pan and set aside.
Add into the pan sprouting broccoli, snow peas, baby corn, carrots and red cabbage and stir-fry for a 3-4 minutes.
Stir in the noodles and sauce and combine with the rest of the ingredients. Add in the garlic and chilli previously set aside and stir-fry for 1-2 minutes, then remove from the pan.
Squeeze the juice of a lime over the noodles, then sprinkle the spring onion, cilantro, and roasted peanuts on top and serve.
Store in an airtight container in the fridge for up to 2 days.

Per serving: Calories: 253; Carbs: 42.54 g; Protein: 9.22 g; Total Fat: 6.93 g; Fiber: 5.8 g; Sugar: 17.33 g; Sodium: 615 mg; Potassium: 640 mg; Calcium (Ca): 105 mg; Vitamin B-12: 0 µg; Vitamin D: 0 IU

Broccoli Pesto Pasta

Prep Time: 10 minutes | **Cook Time:** 20 minutes | **Serves:** 4

Ingredients:
1 head broccoli floret
3 cups short pasta, like paccheri
Handful fresh basil leaves
2-ounce toasted pine nuts
1 garlic clove, grated
Zest of 1 lemon
1 teaspoon fresh lemon juice
4 tablespoons extra-virgin olive oil
Sea salt & cracked black pepper

To Serve:
Toasted pine nuts
Handful of basil leaves
Lemon zest
Cracked black pepper

Directions:
Cook the broccoli florets in a large pot of lightly salted boiling water, for about 5 minutes, or just until tender.
With the help of a slotted spoon, transfer the florets from the water into a bowl with cold water and ice, then drain and set aside.
Fold the pasta into the pot used for cooking the broccoli and cook until al dente, about 10 minutes for paccheri.
Add broccoli florets, basil leaves, pine nuts, garlic, lemon juice and zest into a food processor and pulse until crumbly.
Set the food processor on slow speed and gently pour in the extra-virgin olive oil. Continue to mix until your broccoli pesto reaches a creamy texture.
Add 60 ml (¼ cup) of pasta cooking water into the broccoli pesto and continue to mix until reaching a creamy texture. Season with sea salt and black pepper to time.
Drain the pasta, return to the pot and stir in the broccoli pesto.
Divide the broccoli pesto pasta among 4 plates, top with extra pine nuts, lemon zest, basil leaves and freshy cracked black pepper, and serve.

Per serving: Calories: 299; Carbs: 34.85 g; Protein: 5.92 g; Total Fat: 16.63 g; Fiber: 6.6 g; Sugar: 1.49 g; Sodium: 133 mg; Potassium: 258 mg; Calcium (Ca): 24 mg; Vitamin B-12: 0.02 µg; Vitamin D: 0 IU

Zuppa Toscana

Prep Time: 10 minutes | **Cook Time:** 20 minutes | **Serves:** 4

Ingredients:
1 tablespoon olive oil
1 yellow onion, diced
3-4 medium Yukon gold or russet potatoes, peeled and diced
½ cup sun-dried tomatoes in oil, drained and chopped
1 teaspoon dried oregano
5 sprigs fresh thyme
4 cups vegetable stock
2 cups almond milk, unsweetened
3 cups kale leaves ribs removed, chopped
1 (14-ounce) can cannellini beans
1 tablespoon nutritional yeast
¼ cup fresh parsley chopped
1 tablespoon lemon juice
½ teaspoon red pepper flakes or to time
Salt and pepper
1 teaspoon vegan pesto par portion to serve
Crusty bread to serve

Directions:
Preheat a large heavy bottom pot over medium heat. Add the olive oil and onion and sauté for a few minutes until translucent.
Add diced potatoes and continue cooking for 2-3 minutes, stirring often.
Add sun-dried tomatoes, minced garlic, oregano and thyme and sauté for one more minute. Scrape all the brown bits from the bottom of the pan.
Add vegetable stock and bring to a boil. Cook for almost about 7 minutes, until the potatoes are softened. Add unsweetened almond milk and bring to a boil.
Add kale and cook for almost 5 minutes.
Add cannellini beans, nutritional yeast, parsley and lemon juice (if using).
Sprinkle with chili flakes, salt and pepper to time. Serve with a dollop of vegan pesto and crusty bread on the side. Enjoy!

Per serving: Calories: 384; Carbs: 62.81 g; Protein: 16.02 g; Total Fat: 9.69 g; Fiber: 8.6 g; Sugar: 13.87 g; Sodium: 882 mg; Potassium: 1684 mg; Calcium (Ca): 296 mg; Vitamin B-12: 0.69 µg; Vitamin D: 59 IU

Corn Chowder

Prep Time: 10 minutes | **Cook Time:** 20 minutes | **Serves:** 4

Ingredients:
1 tablespoon olive oil
1 medium-sized onion, chopped
3 ears grilled corn on the cob (or fresh sweet corn, husked)
2 garlic cloves, minced
2-3 small yellow potatoes, diced
1 zucchini, diced
1 yellow bell pepper, diced
3 cups homemade vegetable broth
1 (14 ounces) can light almond milk
1 tablespoon white wine vinegar
1 teaspoon smoked paprika
Pinch of salt
½ teaspoon ground black pepper
5 tablespoons millet
4 tablespoons avocado dill dressing
4 sprigs fresh dill, to garnish

Directions:
In a large pot, heat a lug of olive oil and sauté your onions until translucent. Slice kernels off the corn. Add garlic, diced potatoes, zucchini and bell pepper, corn kernels (saving 4 tablespoons for garnishing), and continue sautéing for about 5 more minutes, stirring occasionally.
Add vegetable broth, almond milk, vinegar, smoked paprika, salt, ground black pepper and millet.
Cover and simmer for 10-15 more minutes, until the potatoes are done.
If it's too thick to your time, thin it up with a bit more vegetable broth.
Pulse half the soup in a blender until smooth and return it back to the pot.
Stir everything well and serve with avocado dill dressing, corn kernels and fresh dill. Enjoy!

Per serving: Calories: 375; Carbs: 70.41 g; Protein: 10.18 g; Total Fat: 7.49 g; Fiber: 8.6 g; Sugar: 13.55 g; Sodium: 689 mg; Potassium: 1152 mg; Calcium (Ca): 249 mg; Vitamin B-12: 1.31 µg; Vitamin D: 42 IU

Chapter 6 Snack Recipes

Mayo Onion and Cauliflower Dip

Prep Time: 20 minutes | **Cook Time:** 30 minutes | **Serves:** 24

Ingredients:
1 ½ cups chicken stock
1 cauliflower head, florets separated
¼ cup olive oil mayonnaise
½ cup yellow onion, chopped
¾ cup cream cheese
½ teaspoon chili powder
½ teaspoon cumin, ground
½ teaspoon garlic powder
Salt and black pepper to the taste

Directions:
In a pot, pour in the stock and add cauliflower and onion. Cook over medium heat about 30 minutes.
Add salt, pepper, cumin, garlic, and chili powder and stir well.
Stir in cream cheese until melt. Then blend in the olive oil mayo until well mixed.
Transfer to a bowl and put in the refrigerator for 2 hours before serving.
Serve and enjoy!

Per serving: Calories: 39; Carbs: 1.49 g; Protein: 1.06 g; Total Fat: 3.28 g; Fiber: 0.3 g; Sugar: 0.74 g; Sodium: 72 mg; Potassium: 59 mg; Calcium (Ca): 9 mg; Vitamin B-12: 0.03 µg; Vitamin D: 2 IU

Basil Pesto Crackers

Prep Time: 10 minutes | **Cook Time:** 17 minutes | **Serves:** 6

Ingredients:
½ teaspoon baking powder
Salt and black pepper to the taste
1¼ cups almond flour
¼ teaspoon basil, dried
1 garlic clove, minced
2 tablespoons basil pesto
A pinch of cayenne pepper
3 tablespoons ghee

Directions:
Prepare a baking sheet and line with parchment paper.
Mix together pepper, baking powder, almond flour, and salt in a bowl.
Then stir in garlic, basil, and cayenne and mix well.
Whisk in the basil pesto and then add ghee. Knead the dough.
Arrange the dough on the prepared baking sheet and bake in your oven at 325 degrees F for 17 minutes.
When cooked, set it aside to cool and cut into your desired size.
Serve and enjoy!

Per serving: Calories: 57; Carbs: 1.18 g; Protein: 0.33 g; Total Fat: 5.91 g; Fiber: 0.2 g; Sugar: 0.41 g; Sodium: 2 mg; Potassium: 77 mg; Calcium (Ca): 25 mg; Vitamin B-12: 0.01 µg; Vitamin D: 4 IU

Zucchini Taco Boats

Prep Time: 20 minutes | **Cook Time:** 70 minutes | **Serves:** 4

Ingredients:
4 medium zucchinis, cut in half lengthwise
¼ cup fresh cilantro, chopped
½ cup cheddar cheese, shredded
¼ cup water
4-ounce tomato sauce
2 tablespoons bell pepper, mined
½ small onion, minced
½ teaspoon oregano
1 teaspoon paprika
1 teaspoon chili powder
1 teaspoon cumin
1 teaspoon garlic powder
1-pound lean ground turkey
½ cup salsa
1 teaspoon kosher salt

Directions:
At 400 degrees F, preheat your oven. Add ¼ cup salsa in the bottom of the baking dish.
Using a spoon, hollow out the center of the zucchini halves. Chop the scooped-out flesh of zucchini and set aside ¾ of a cup chopped meat. Add zucchini halves to the boiling water and cook for almost 1 minute. Remove zucchini halves from water.
Add ground turkey in a suitable pan and cook until meat is no longer pink. Add spices and mix well. Add reserved zucchini flesh, water, tomato sauce, bell pepper, and onion.
Stir well and cover, simmer over low heat for 20 minutes. Stuff zucchini boats with taco meat and top each with one tablespoon of shredded cheddar cheese. Place zucchini boats in a baking dish. Cover this dish with foil and bake in preheated oven for 35 minutes. Top with remaining salsa and chopped cilantro. Serve and enjoy.

Per serving: Calories: 189; Carbs: 9.4 g; Protein: 30.68 g; Total Fat: 4 g; Fiber: 2 g; Sugar: 3.95 g; Sodium: 1055 mg; Potassium: 727 mg; Calcium (Ca): 117 mg; Vitamin B-12: 0.74 µg; Vitamin D: 16 IU

Creamy Kiwi Smoothie

Prep Time: 5 minutes | **Cook Time:** 3 minutes | **Serves:** 4

Ingredients:
5 kiwis, pulp scooped
2 tablespoons erythritol
2 cups almond milk
2 cups coconut cream
7 ice cubes
Mint leaves to garnish

Directions:
In a blender, process the kiwis, erythritol, milk, cream, and ice cubes until smooth, about 3 minutes.
Pour into four serving glasses, garnish with mint leaves, and serve.

Per serving: Calories: 335; Carbs: 29.82 g; Protein: 5.84 g; Total Fat: 22.68 g; Fiber: 1.3 g; Sugar: 28.8 g; Sodium: 80 mg; Potassium: 375 mg; Calcium (Ca): 198 mg; Vitamin B-12: 0.67 µg; Vitamin D: 16 IU

Cashew Milk

Prep Time: 5 minutes | **Cook Time:** Overnight to soak | **Serves:** 8

Ingredients:
4 cups water
¼ cup raw cashews, soaked overnight

Directions:
In a blender, blend the water and cashews at high speed for 2 minutes.
Strain with a nut-milk bag or cheesecloth, then stores in the refrigerator for up to 5 days.
Tip: This recipe makes unsweetened cashew milk that can be used in savory and sweet dishes.
For a creamier version to put in your coffee, cut the amount of water in half.
For a sweeter version, add 1 to 2 tablespoons maple syrup and 1 teaspoon vanilla extract before blending.

Per serving: Calories: 49; Carbs: 2.42 g; Protein: 0.97 g; Total Fat: 4.24 g; Fiber: 0.2 g; Sugar: 0.73 g; Sodium: 26 mg; Potassium: 36 mg; Calcium (Ca): 17 mg; Vitamin B-12: 0 µg; Vitamin D: 0 IU

Orange Juice Soda

Prep Time: 5 minutes | **Cook Time:** 30 minutes | **Serves:** 4

Ingredients:
4 cups carbonated water
2 cups pulp-free orange juice (4 oranges, and strained)

Directions:
For each serving, pour 2 parts carbonated water and 1 part orange juice over ice right before serving.
Stir and enjoy.

Per serving: Calories: 56; Carbs: 12.9 g; Protein: 0.87 g; Total Fat: 0.25 g; Fiber: 0.2 g; Sugar: 10.42 g; Sodium: 6 mg; Potassium: 248 mg; Calcium (Ca): 37 mg; Vitamin B-12: 0 µg; Vitamin D: 0 IU

Oat Milk

Prep Time: 5 minutes | **Cook Time:** 15 minutes | **Serves:** 8

Ingredients:
1 cup rolled oats
4 cups water

Directions:
Put the oats in a suitable bowl, and cover with cold water. Soak for 15 minutes, then drain and rinse the oats.
Pour the cold water and the soaked oats into a blender. Blend for 60 to 90 seconds, or just until the mixture is a creamy white color throughout. (Blending any further may over blend the oats, resulting in a gummy milk.)
Strain through a nut-milk bag or colander, then store in the refrigerator for up to 5 days.

Per serving: Calories: 29; Carbs: 7.78 g; Protein: 2.03 g; Total Fat: 0.83 g; Fiber: 1.8 g; Sugar: 0.17 g; Sodium: 3 mg; Potassium: 67 mg; Calcium (Ca): 19 mg; Vitamin B-12: 0 µg; Vitamin D: 0 IU

Creamy Caramel Cones

Prep Time: 25 minutes | **Cook Time:** 2 hours | **Serves:** 6

Ingredients:
2 tablespoons heavy whipping cream
2 tablespoons sour cream
1 tablespoon caramel sugar
1 teaspoon sea salt, fine
⅓ cup butter, grass-fed
⅓ cup coconut oil
Stevia to taste

Directions:
Mix together the softened coconut oil and butter.
Add the remaining ingredients in the mixture to make a batter.
Divide into molds and add a little salt on the top.
Put in the refrigerator before serving.
Serve and enjoy!

Per serving: Calories: 265; Carbs: 2.11 g; Protein: 0.42 g; Total Fat: 29.26 g; Fiber: 0 g; Sugar: 1.75 g; Sodium: 568 mg; Potassium: 18 mg; Calcium (Ca): 15 mg; Vitamin B-12: 0.06 µg; Vitamin D: 11 IU

Stuffed Eggs

Prep Time: 2 hours and 10 minutes | **Cook Time:** 7 minutes | **Serves:** 4

Ingredients:
6 eggs
1 and ¼ cups water
¼ cup unsweetened rice vinegar
2 tablespoons coconut aminos
Salt and black pepper to the taste
2 garlic cloves, minced
1 teaspoon stevia
4 ounces' cream cheese
1 tablespoon chives, chopped

Directions:
In a pot, place the eggs and then pour water to cover. Bring to a boil over medium heat for about 7 minutes.
Under cold water, rinse the eggs and set it aside to cool.
Mix 1 cup of water, vinegar, garlic, and stevia in a bowl until well whisked.
Add the eggs in the bowl. Cover with a kitchen towel and set aside for 2 hours, rotating occasionally.
Peel the boiled eggs and cut in halves. In a bowl, add the yolks.
Then stir in ¼ cup of water, salt, cream cheese, pepper, and chives until well combined.
Add the mixture into the egg whites.
Serve and enjoy!

Per serving: Calories: 185; Carbs: 2.68 g; Protein: 10.48 g; Total Fat: 14.41 g; Fiber: 0.1 g; Sugar: 1.52 g; Sodium: 227 mg; Potassium: 161 mg; Calcium (Ca): 69 mg; Vitamin B-12: 0.91 µg; Vitamin D: 60 IU

Pumpkin Spiced Donuts

Prep Time: 10 minutes | **Cook Time:** 25 minutes | **Serves:** 8

Ingredients:
1 cup oat flour
¾ cup xylitol
1 scoop, powdered vanilla protein
1 tablespoon ground flaxseed
1 tablespoon ground cinnamon
2 teaspoons baking powder
1 teaspoon sea salt
3 beaten eggs
½ cup, canned pumpkin
1 tablespoon canola oil
2 teaspoons vanilla, pure
1 teaspoon apple cider vinegar
Ingredients for the frosting:
½ cup cream cheese, whipped
½ teaspoon liquid swerve

Directions:
Place the xylitol, oat flour, ground flaxseed, powdered protein, baking powder, ground cinnamon, and a dash of sea salt in a suitable bowl. Preheat your oven to 350 degrees Fahrenheit.
Add the egg (beaten) into another bowl (large) along with the pumpkin (canned), pure vanilla and vinegar, and canola oil (melted).
Whisk until mixed evenly, then pour the mixture into the flour. Stir until thoroughly mixed.
Using cooking spray, grease a suitable donut pan.
Pour batter into a greased donut pan.
Place batter into the oven and bake for approximately 10 minutes until thoroughly baked.
Remove from heat and set donuts onto a wire rack to cool.
Add in whipped cream cheese and liquid swerve in a small bowl, whisk until smooth.
Frost donuts using the frosting and serve with a sprinkle of ground cinnamon over the top.

Per serving: Calories: 200; Carbs: 13.93 g; Protein: 7.62 g; Total Fat: 13.07 g; Fiber: 2.2 g; Sugar: 2.73 g; Sodium: 404 mg; Potassium: 294 mg; Calcium (Ca): 102 mg; Vitamin B-12: 0.22 µg; Vitamin D: 17 IU

Roasted Seeds

Prep Time: 5 minutes | **Cook Time:** 30 minutes | **Serves:** 4

Ingredients:
½ cup sunflower seeds
2 tablespoons nutritional yeast
½ teaspoon garlic powder

Directions:
In a suitable blender, blend nutritional yeast, the sunflower seeds, and garlic powder.
Blend on low speed for 30 to 45 seconds, or until the sunflower seeds have been broken down.
Store in a secure container in the refrigerator for up to 2 months.

Per serving: Calories: 120; Carbs: 5.63 g; Protein: 5.85 g; Total Fat: 9.09 g; Fiber: 2.1 g; Sugar: 0.61 g; Sodium: 268 mg; Potassium: 307 mg; Calcium (Ca): 20 mg; Vitamin B-12: 0.05 µg; Vitamin D: 0 IU

Asian Noodle Salad

Prep Time: 20 minutes | **Cook Time:** 5 minutes | **Serves:** 12

Ingredients:
1 pack Whole wheat noodles
24-ounce broccoli
5 grated carrots
¼ cup extra virgin olive oil
⅕ cup rice vinegar
4 tablespoons of honey
4 tablespoons of creamy butter
1 tablespoon smashed garlic
¾ cup roasted peanuts chopped

Directions:
First, you have to cook and drain the noodles. If you are using soba noodles, you should add a tablespoon of salt to your water and salt won't be necessary when using Chinese noodles.
After draining the noodles, rinse with cold water and then spread out the noodles on a suitable pan to dry.
Steam the broccoli by viding it in boiled water and steam for about 4 minutes, rinse with cold water, and set aside.
In your mixing bowl, whisk together the olive or cooking oil, honey, rice vinegar, your creamy butter, and garlic.
Pour it inside the noodle and toss.
Then add the roasted peanuts at this point and toss it again.
Serve chilled or at room temperature.

Per serving: Calories: 242; Carbs: 27.5 g; Protein: 9.03 g; Total Fat: 12.46 g; Fiber: 4.4 g; Sugar: 9.2 g; Sodium: 271 mg; Potassium: 343 mg; Calcium (Ca): 85 mg; Vitamin B-12: 0.01 µg; Vitamin D: 3 IU

Cinnamon Bites

Prep Time: 20 minutes | **Cook Time:** 95 minutes | **Serves:** 6

Ingredients:
⅛ teaspoon nutmeg
1 teaspoon vanilla extract
¼ teaspoon cinnamon
4 tablespoons coconut oil
½ cup butter, grass-fed
8 ounces' cream cheese
Stevia to taste

Directions:
In a bowl, add cream cheese, and soften coconut oil and butter.
Add the remaining ingredients in the bowl and mix well.
Divide the mixture into molds and put in the freezer until set.
Serve and enjoy!

Per serving: Calories: 328; Carbs: 1.54 g; Protein: 2.85 g; Total Fat: 35.24 g; Fiber: 0.1 g; Sugar: 1.43 g; Sodium: 167 mg; Potassium: 49 mg; Calcium (Ca): 33 mg; Vitamin B-12: 0.18 µg; Vitamin D: 19 IU

Vegan Marinara

Prep Time: 5 minutes | **Cook Time:** 15 minutes | **Serves:** 2

Ingredients:
1 cup water
1 cup tomato paste
2 tablespoons maple syrup
1 teaspoon dried oregano
1 teaspoon dried thyme
1 teaspoon garlic powder
1 teaspoon onion powder
½ teaspoon dried basil
¼ teaspoon red pepper flakes

Directions:
In a suitable saucepan, bring the water to a rolling boil over high heat.
Reduce its heat to low, and whisk in the tomato paste, maple syrup, oregano, thyme, garlic powder, basil, onion powder, and red pepper flakes.
Cover and simmer for 10 minutes, stirring occasionally. Serve warm.

Per serving: Calories: 174; Carbs: 41.52 g; Protein: 6.32 g; Total Fat: 0.7 g; Fiber: 6.2 g; Sugar: 28.6 g; Sodium: 85 mg; Potassium: 1444 mg; Calcium (Ca): 101 mg; Vitamin B-12: 0 µg; Vitamin D: 0 IU

Pumpkin Muffins

Prep Time: 10 minutes | **Cook Time:** 15 minutes | **Serves:** 18

Ingredients:
¼ cup sunflower seed butter
¾ cup pumpkin puree
2 tablespoons flaxseed meal
¼ cup coconut flour
½ cup erythritol
½ teaspoon nutmeg, ground
1 teaspoon cinnamon, ground
½ teaspoon baking soda
1 egg
½ teaspoon baking powder
A pinch of salt

Directions:
Mix butter, egg, and pumpkin puree in a bowl and blend well.
Add coconut flour, erythritol, baking soda, baking powder, cinnamon, a pinch of salt, flaxseed meal, and nutmeg and stir well.
Then spoon the mixture into a greased muffin pan and cook in your oven at 350 degrees F for 15 minutes.
When cooked, set the muffins aside to cool.
Serve and enjoy!

Per serving: Calories: 64; Carbs: 2.9 g; Protein: 2.63 g; Total Fat: 5.12 g; Fiber: 1 g; Sugar: 1.22 g; Sodium: 52 mg; Potassium: 95 mg; Calcium (Ca): 18 mg; Vitamin B-12: 0.02 µg; Vitamin D: 2 IU

Coconut Fat Bombs

Prep Time: 2 minutes | **Cook Time:** 10 minutes | **Serves:** 8

Ingredients:
⅔ cup canola oil
1 (14 ounces) can almond milk
18 drops swerve liquid
1 cup unsweetened coconut flakes

Directions:
Mix the canola oil with the milk and swerve to combine.
Stir in the coconut flakes until well distributed.
Pour into silicone muffin molds and freeze for 1 hour to harden.

Per serving: Calories: 235; Carbs: 11.47 g; Protein: 0.37 g; Total Fat: 21.35 g; Fiber: 1.1 g; Sugar: 9.19 g; Sodium: 31 mg; Potassium: 40 mg; Calcium (Ca): 2 mg; Vitamin B-12: 0 µg; Vitamin D: 0 IU

Tomato Avocado Salad

Prep Time: 5 minutes | **Cook Time:** 15 minutes | **Serves:** 4

Ingredients:
12-ounce cherry tomatoes, cut in half
5 small cucumbers, chopped
3 small avocados, chopped
½ teaspoon ground black pepper
2 tablespoons olive oil
2 tablespoons fresh lemon juice
¼ cup fresh cilantro, chopped
1 teaspoon sea salt

Directions:
Add cherry tomatoes, cucumbers, avocados, and cilantro into the large mixing bowl and mix well.
Mix olive oil, lemon juice, black pepper, and salt and pour over salad.
Toss well and serve immediately.

Per serving: Calories: 287; Carbs: 28.89 g; Protein: 6.69 g; Total Fat: 19.05 g; Fiber: 11.9 g; Sugar: 15.18 g; Sodium: 614 mg; Potassium: 1712 mg; Calcium (Ca): 85 mg; Vitamin B-12: 0 µg; Vitamin D: 0 IU

Almond Chocolate Bites

Prep Time: 30 minutes | **Cook Time:** 90 minutes | **Serves:** 12

Ingredients:
2 cups butter, grass-fed
2 ounces' heavy cream
½ cup Stevia
⅔ cup cocoa powder
1 teaspoon vanilla extract, pure
4 tablespoons almond butter

Directions:
With the help of double boiler, melt your butter.
Mix together all the ingredients.
Place the prepared mixture into molds.
Freeze the molds for 2 hours.

Per serving: Calories: 274; Carbs: 3.02 g; Protein: 2.41 g; Total Fat: 29.65 g; Fiber: 1.4 g; Sugar: 0.26 g; Sodium: 19 mg; Potassium: 156 mg; Calcium (Ca): 30 mg; Vitamin B-12: 0.07 µg; Vitamin D: 21 IU

Watermelon Lemonade

Prep Time: 5 minutes | **Cook Time:** 30 minutes | **Serves:** 6

Ingredients:
4 cups diced watermelon
4 cups cold water
2 tablespoons lemon juice
1 tablespoon lime juice

Directions:
In a blender, combine the watermelon, water, lemon juice, and lime juice, and blend for 1 minute.
Strain the contents through a fine-mesh sieve or nut-milk bag. Serve chilled.
Store in the refrigerator for up to 3 days.

Per serving: Calories: 33; Carbs: 8.31 g; Protein: 0.65 g; Total Fat: 0.17 g; Fiber: 0.4 g; Sugar: 6.54 g; Sodium: 4 mg; Potassium: 123 mg; Calcium (Ca): 24 mg; Vitamin B-12: 0 µg; Vitamin D: 0 IU

Chapter 7 Dessert Recipes

Rhubarb Delight

Prep Time: 5 minutes | **Cook Time:** 5 minutes | **Serves:** 2

Ingredients:
3 cups rhubarb, chopped
1 tablespoon ghee, melted
⅓ cup water
1 tablespoon stevia
1 teaspoon vanilla extract

Directions:
In your Instant Pot, add all the ingredients.
Cover the lid and set the Instant Pot on Pressure function.
Cook on High pressure for about 5 minutes.
Then divide the mixture into small serving bowls.
Serve and enjoy!

Per serving: Calories: 95; Carbs: 9.08 g; Protein: 1.71 g; Total Fat: 6.13 g; Fiber: 3.3 g; Sugar: 2.28 g; Sodium: 9 mg; Potassium: 532 mg; Calcium (Ca): 163 mg; Vitamin B-12: 0.01 µg; Vitamin D: 4 IU

Lemony Raspberry Compote

Prep Time: 12 minutes | **Cook Time:** 30 minutes | **Serves:** 2

Ingredients:
1 cup raspberries
½ cup Swerve
1 teaspoon freshly grated lemon zest
1 teaspoon vanilla extract
2 cups water

Directions:
Set your Instant Pot on Sauté function.
Add all the ingredients in the pot and stir well. Pour in 1 cup of water.
Cook for about 5 minutes, stirring continually, and then pour 1 more cup of water. Turn off heat.
Properly secure the lid, then set the Instant Pot on Manual function. Set time to 15 minutes on Low pressure.
When time is up, turn off the heat and naturally release the pressure, about 10 minutes.
Then turn the pressure valve to Venting position and open the lid.
Allow it sit to cool. Serve and enjoy!

Per serving: Calories: 209; Carbs: 49.79 g; Protein: 0.8 g; Total Fat: 0.65 g; Fiber: 4.1 g; Sugar: 40.46 g; Sodium: 8 mg; Potassium: 101 mg; Calcium (Ca): 40 mg; Vitamin B-12: 0 µg; Vitamin D: 0 IU

Banana Bread

Prep Time: 5 minutes | **Cook Time:** 40 minutes | **Serves:** 3

Ingredients:
¾ cup swerve
⅓ cup butter
1 tablespoon vanilla extract
1 egg
3 ripe bananas
1 tablespoon baking powder
1 ½ cups flour
½ tablespoon baking soda
⅓ cup milk
1 ½ tablespoons cream of tartar
Cooking spray

Directions:
Mix in milk with cream of tartar, vanilla, egg, swerve, bananas, and butter in a container and turn whole.
Mix in flour with baking soda and baking powder.
Blend the 2 mixtures, turn properly and move into oiled skillet with cooking spray. Put into the air fryer, and cook at 320 degrees F for 40 minutes.
Remove bread, allow to cool, slice.
Serve.

Per serving: Calories: 522; Carbs: 81.69 g; Protein: 11.25 g; Total Fat: 16.87 g; Fiber: 4.9 g; Sugar: 16.56 g; Sodium: 680 mg; Potassium: 1816 mg; Calcium (Ca): 283 mg; Vitamin B-12: 0.28 µg; Vitamin D: 22 IU

Custard Filled Pears

Prep Time: 10 minutes | **Cook Time:** 10 minutes | **Serves:** 4

Ingredients:
1 puff pastry sheets
14-ounce vanilla custard
2 pears
1 egg
½ tablespoon cinnamon powder
4 tablespoons swerve

Directions:
Put wisp pastry slices on a flat surface, add a spoonful of vanilla custard at the middle of each, add pear halves and wrap.
Sweep pears with egg and cinnamon. Drizzle swerve on top, put into air fryer's basket, and cook at 320 degrees F for 15 minutes.
Split parcels on plates.
Serve.

Per serving: Calories: 251; Carbs: 48.17 g; Protein: 4.28 g; Total Fat: 6.33 g; Fiber: 5.3 g; Sugar: 13.8 g; Sodium: 49 mg; Potassium: 480 mg; Calcium (Ca): 49 mg; Vitamin B-12: 0.1 µg; Vitamin D: 9 IU

Lime Poached Pears

Prep Time: 10 minutes | **Cook Time:** 10 minutes | **Serves:** 2

Ingredients:
1 tablespoon lime juice
2 teaspoons lime zest
1 cinnamon stick
2 whole pears, peeled
1 cup water
Fresh mint leaves

Directions:
In the Instant Pot, add lime juice, lime zest, cinnamon stick, the peeled pears, and 1 cup of water.
Then set the Instant Pot on Manual and then cook on high for 10 minutes.
When cooked, release the pressure naturally.
Then carefully remove the pears from the pot and transfer to serving bowls.
Add the fresh mint leaves to garnish.
Serve and enjoy!

Per serving: Calories: 58; Carbs: 15.11 g; Protein: 0.72 g; Total Fat: 0.31 g; Fiber: 5.1 g; Sugar: 8.84 g; Sodium: 3 mg; Potassium: 169 mg; Calcium (Ca): 32 mg; Vitamin B-12: 0 µg; Vitamin D: 0 IU

Cinnamon Banana Cake

Prep Time: 11 minutes | **Cook Time:** 30 minutes | **Serves:** 4

Ingredients:
1 tablespoon butter
1 egg
⅓ cup brown sugar
2 tablespoons honey
1 banana
1 cup white flour
1 tablespoon baking powder
½ tablespoon cinnamon powder
Cooking spray, to grease

Directions:
Prepare a suitable cake pan and spray with cooking spray.
In a bowl, add sugar, honey, cinnamon, banana, egg, baking powder, flour, and butter together and whisk well.
Pour the mixture onto the prepared cake pan and cook in the air fryer at 350 degrees F for about 30 minutes.
Let it sit to cool. Then slice into your desired size.
Serve and enjoy!

Per serving: Calories: 288; Carbs: 59.67 g; Protein: 5.06 g; Total Fat: 4.36 g; Fiber: 2.2 g; Sugar: 29.99 g; Sodium: 26 mg; Potassium: 568 mg; Calcium (Ca): 201 mg; Vitamin B-12: 0.1 µg; Vitamin D: 11 IU

Creamy Cheesecake

Prep Time: 12 minutes | **Cook Time:** 15 minutes | **Serves:** 15

Ingredients:
1-pound cream cheese
½ tablespoon vanilla extract
2 eggs
4 tablespoons sugar
1 cup graham crackers
2 tablespoons butter

Directions:
In a suitable bowl, mix together the butter and crackers.
Then compress the mixture to the bottom cake pan.
Put into your air fryer and cook at 350 degrees F for about 4 minutes.
In a suitable bowl, add cream cheese, sugar, vanilla, and the beaten egg and beat properly.
Sprinkle the mixture onto the crackers and cook the cheesecake in the air fryer at 310 degrees F for about 15 minutes.
Then put in the fridge for about 3 hours. Slice into your desired size.
Serve and enjoy!

Per serving: Calories: 122; Carbs: 3.42 g; Protein: 2.91 g; Total Fat: 10.8 g; Fiber: 0 g; Sugar: 3.24 g; Sodium: 142 mg; Potassium: 40 mg; Calcium (Ca): 26 mg; Vitamin B-12: 0.18 µg; Vitamin D: 12 IU

Cherry Bread Pudding

Prep Time: 10 minutes | **Cook Time:** 10 minutes | **Serves:** 4

Ingredients:
6 glazed doughnuts
1 cup cherries
4 egg yolks
1 and ½ cups whipping cream
½ cup raisins
¼ cup sugar
½ cup chocolate chips

Directions:
In a suitable bowl, mix the cherries with the yolks and whipping cream and then turn properly.
In a separate bowl, add raisins, chocolate chips, doughnuts, and sugar and mix well.
Prepare a baking pan and grease with cooking spray.
Mix these two mixture together and transfer onto the prepared the baking pan.
Put the pan in your air fryer and cook at 310 degrees F for about 1 hour.
Allow it to cool. Then cut into your desired size.
Serve and enjoy!

Per serving: Calories: 567; Carbs: 62.81 g; Protein: 12.47 g; Total Fat: 29.81 g; Fiber: 2.9 g; Sugar: 35.35 g; Sodium: 380 mg; Potassium: 271 mg; Calcium (Ca): 140 mg; Vitamin B-12: 0.54 µg; Vitamin D: 41 IU

Dark Chocolate Cherry Cookies

Prep Time: 16 minutes | **Cook Time:** 12 minutes | **Serves:** 2

Ingredients:
1 lean-and-green dark chocolate cherry shake
½ teaspoon baking powder
2 tablespoons water

Directions:
Prepare a baking sheet and line over with parchment paper.
Before cooking, heat your oven to 350 degrees F.
In a suitable bowl, mix together the baking powder, water, and cherry shake together to make a form.
Divide the batter onto the prepared baking sheet, into 8 small cookies.
Then in the preheated oven, bake the cookies for 12 minutes.
Serve and enjoy!

Per serving: Calories: 303; Carbs: 23.77 g; Protein: 3.94 g; Total Fat: 21.53 g; Fiber: 5.5 g; Sugar: 12.11 g; Sodium: 12 mg; Potassium: 487 mg; Calcium (Ca): 92 mg; Vitamin B-12: 0.14 µg; Vitamin D: 0 IU

Banana Cake

Prep Time: 10 minutes | **Cook Time:** 30 minutes | **Serves:** 3

Ingredients:
½ cup butter, soft
2 eggs
⅓ cup brown swerve
1 tablespoon honey
1 banana
1 cup white flour
1 tablespoon baking powder
½ tablespoon cinnamon powder
Cooking spray

Directions:
Spray cake skillet with cooking spray.
Add in butter with egg, swerve, banana, cinnamon, honey, flour, and baking powder in a container then beat.
Pour batter into cake pan filled with cooking spray, place in a deep fryer, and cook at 350 degrees F for 30 minutes.
Let cool, cut into slices.
Serve.

Per serving: Calories: 402; Carbs: 55.42 g; Protein: 7.32 g; Total Fat: 17.95 g; Fiber: 2.2 g; Sugar: 25.72 g; Sodium: 51 mg; Potassium: 599 mg; Calcium (Ca): 220 mg; Vitamin B-12: 0.23 µg; Vitamin D: 29 IU

Mini Lava Cakes

Prep Time: 5 minutes | **Cook Time:** 20 minutes | **Serves:** 3

Ingredients:
2 large eggs
2 tablespoons swerve
4 tablespoons olive oil
¼ cup milk
1 teaspoon flour
⅛ cup cocoa powder
½ tablespoon baking powder
½ tablespoon orange zest

Directions:
Mix in egg with swerve, flour, salt, oil, milk, orange zest, baking powder, and cocoa powder, turn properly. Move it to oiled ramekins.
Put ramekins in an air fryer and cook at 320 degrees F for 20 minutes.
Serve warm.

Per serving: Calories: 257; Carbs: 12.56 g; Protein: 5.67 g; Total Fat: 21.74 g; Fiber: 1.2 g; Sugar: 7.68 g; Sodium: 60 mg; Potassium: 430 mg; Calcium (Ca): 157 mg; Vitamin B-12: 0.4 µg; Vitamin D: 37 IU

Apple Bread

Prep Time: 5 minutes | **Cook Time:** 40 minutes | **Serves:** 5

Ingredients:
3 cup apples
1 cup swerve
1 tablespoon vanilla
2 eggs
1 tablespoon apple pie spice
2 cups white flour
1 tablespoon baking powder
1 stick butter
1 cup water

Directions:
Mix in egg with 1 butter stick, swerve, and apple pie spice and turn using a mixer.
Put apples and turn properly.
Mix baking powder with flour in another container and turn.
Blend the 2 mixtures, turn and move them to the spring-form skillet.
Get the spring-form skillet into an air fryer and cook at 320 degrees F for 40 minutes
Slice into your desired size and serve.

Per serving: Calories: 201; Carbs: 39.15 g; Protein: 5.06 g; Total Fat: 2.45 g; Fiber: 2.5 g; Sugar: 14.83 g; Sodium: 31 mg; Potassium: 436 mg; Calcium (Ca): 160 mg; Vitamin B-12: 0.16 µg; Vitamin D: 15 IU

Bread Dough in Amaretto

Prep Time: 16 minutes | **Cook Time:** 8 minutes | **Serves:** 12

Ingredients:
1-pound bread dough, cut into 40 half slices
1 cup sugar
½ cup butter
1 cup heavy cream
12 ounces' chocolate chips
2 tablespoons amaretto liqueur

Directions:
Sweep the spray sugar and butter over the dough pieces and then transfer into the air fryer basket. Cook at 350 degrees F for about 5 minutes.
Flip and cook again for 3 minutes. Then transfer to a platter.
In a pan, melt the heavy cream over medium heat and then add the chocolate chips, turning until melt.
Add in the liqueur and turn. Then transfer the chips into a serving bowl.
Serve with your favored sauce.

Per serving: Calories: 385; Carbs: 47.17 g; Protein: 5.08 g; Total Fat: 19.65 g; Fiber: 1.6 g; Sugar: 21.02 g; Sodium: 279 mg; Potassium: 107 mg; Calcium (Ca): 69 mg; Vitamin B-12: 0.04 µg; Vitamin D: 8 IU

Cherry Cream

Prep Time: 14 minutes | **Cook Time:** 0 minutes | **Serves:** 4

Ingredients:
2 cups lite whipped topping, thawed
1 (8-ounce) package cream cheese, softened
1 package sugar-free cherry gelatin
½ cup boiling water

Directions:
In a suitable bowl, whisk the cream cheese with the lite whipped topping until smooth.
In a separate bowl, mix the cherry gelatin with the boiling water.
Mix together the cream mixture with the gelatin mixture until well combined.
Then spread the mixture into a pie pan and cover.
Put in the refrigerator for almost 2 hours.
Serve and enjoy!

Per serving: Calories: 295; Carbs: 10.83 g; Protein: 11.14 g; Total Fat: 21.14 g; Fiber: 0 g; Sugar: 10.83 g; Sodium: 288 mg; Potassium: 102 mg; Calcium (Ca): 71 mg; Vitamin B-12: 0.3 µg; Vitamin D: 12 IU

Bread Cherry Pudding

Prep Time: 10 minutes | **Cook Time:** 60 minutes | **Serves:** 4

Ingredients:
1 oz. glazed doughnuts
2 cups cherries
6 egg yolks
½ cup whipping cream
½ cup raisins
¼ cup swerve
½ cup chocolate chips

Directions:
Add cherries with whipping cream and egg in a container then turn properly.
Combine in raisins with chocolate chips, doughnuts, and swerve in a container, then stir.
Mix the 2 mixtures, pour into the oiled skillet then into the air fryer and cook at 310 degrees F for 1 hour.
Cool pudding before cutting.
Serve.

Per serving: Calories: 239; Carbs: 29.83 g; Protein: 5.84 g; Total Fat: 11.17 g; Fiber: 1.6 g; Sugar: 22.7 g; Sodium: 63 mg; Potassium: 136 mg; Calcium (Ca): 56 mg; Vitamin B-12: 0.53 µg; Vitamin D: 57 IU

Cinnamon-flavored Wrapped Pears

Prep Time: 10| **Cook Time:** 10 minutes | **Serves:** 4

Ingredients:
4 puff pastry sheets
14 ounces' vanilla custard
2 pears
1 egg
½ tablespoon cinnamon powder
2 tablespoons sugar

Directions:
On a flat surface, arrange wisp pastry slices and then at the center of each slice, add spoonful of vanilla custard and pear halves. Wrap.
Sweep egg, cinnamon, and spray sugar over the wrapped pears.
Then put into the air fryer and cook at 320 degrees F for about 15 minutes.
Serve and enjoy!

Per serving: Calories: 419; Carbs: 57.55 g; Protein: 6.84 g; Total Fat: 19.7 g; Fiber: 5.8 g; Sugar: 8.62 g; Sodium: 137 mg; Potassium: 501 mg; Calcium (Ca): 53 mg; Vitamin B-12: 0.1 µg; Vitamin D: 9 IU

Crusted Bananas

Prep Time: 5 minutes | **Cook Time:** 10 minutes | **Serves:** 4

Ingredients:
1 tablespoon butter
2 eggs
2 bananas
½ cup corn flour
1 teaspoon cinnamon
1 cup Panko

Directions:
Preheat a skillet with the butter over medium heat. Put the Panko, turn and cook for almost 4 minutes; then move to a container.
Spin each in flour, Panko, egg blend, assemble them in air fryer's basket, sprinkle with cinnamon and cook at 280 degrees F for 10 minutes.
Serve immediately.

Per serving: Calories: 270; Carbs: 44.83 g; Protein: 8.08 g; Total Fat: 7.17 g; Fiber: 4.2 g; Sugar: 9.08 g; Sodium: 253 mg; Potassium: 344 mg; Calcium (Ca): 73 mg; Vitamin B-12: 0.3 µg; Vitamin D: 20 IU

Minty Yogurt

Prep Time: 5 minutes | **Cook Time:** 10 minutes | **Serves:** 1

Ingredients:
1 cup water
1 cup milk
¾ cup plain yogurt
¼ cup fresh mint
1 tablespoons maple syrup

Directions:
Put 1 cup water into the Instant Pot Pressure Cooker.
Press the "Steam" function button and adjust to 1 minute.
Once done, add the milk, then press the "Yogurt" function button and allow boiling.
Add yogurt and fresh mint, then stir well.
Pour into a glass and add maple syrup.
Enjoy.

Per serving: Calories: 249; Carbs: 34.28 g; Protein: 14.83 g; Total Fat: 6.22 g; Fiber: 0.1 g; Sugar: 33.15 g; Sodium: 195 mg; Potassium: 727 mg; Calcium (Ca): 576 mg; Vitamin B-12: 1.91 µg; Vitamin D: 119 IU

Chocolate Peanut Butter Cups

Prep Time: 16 minutes | **Cook Time:** 12 minutes | **Serves:** 4

Ingredients:
¼ cup creamy peanut butter
5 ounces' chocolate
Cacao Nibs, Sea Salt

Directions:
Put the chocolate and peanut butter in a bowl in your microwave to melt and mix well.
Divide the chocolate mixture into 12 mini muffin cups and cover.
Put in the refrigerator for almost 1 hour.
Serve and enjoy!

Per serving: Calories: 293; Carbs: 21.33 g; Protein: 6.98 g; Total Fat: 21.1 g; Fiber: 2.4 g; Sugar: 15.75 g; Sodium: 119 mg; Potassium: 268 mg; Calcium (Ca): 67 mg; Vitamin B-12: 0.22 µg; Vitamin D: 0 IU

Chocolate Fondue

Prep Time: 5 minutes | **Cook Time:** 10 minutes | **Serves:** 3

Ingredients:
1 cup water
½ teaspoon swerve
½ cup coconut cream
¾ cup dark chocolate, chopped

Directions:
Pour the water into your Instant Pot.
To a heatproof bowl, add the chocolate, swerve, and coconut cream.
Place in the Instant Pot.
Seal the lid, select MANUAL, and cook for almost 2 minutes. When ready, do a quick release and carefully open the lid. Stir well and serve immediately.

Per serving: Calories: 217; Carbs: 12.88 g; Protein: 2.15 g; Total Fat: 19.02 g; Fiber: 1.9 g; Sugar: 8.36 g; Sodium: 6 mg; Potassium: 197 mg; Calcium (Ca): 19 mg; Vitamin B-12: 0.02 µg; Vitamin D: 0 IU

Conclusion

The Lean and Green Diet offers healthy life with various kinds of health benefits. The diet works on three different plans choose the perfect plan as per your needs. It contains lean and green meals with 5 or 6 mini-meals. These mini-meals are called fueling which helps to balance the essential vitamins, minerals, and nutrients in daily diet. The Lean and Green Diet is restrictive and promotes the use of fueling to fulfill the daily nutritional needs. These feelings are nutritionally balanced and scientifically design for better results. The diet is low in carbs and calories it is recommended to consume no more than 1000 calories per day. The lean protein helps you to feel full and also control your calorie intake. Most people follow this diet for effective weight loss purposes. It is recommended to do daily 30 minutes of moderate-intensity exercise to achieve the weight loss goal.

Appendix Measurement Conversion Chart

VOLUME EQUIVALENTS (LIQUID)

US STANDARD	US STANDARD (OUNCES)	METRIC (APPROXIMATE)
2 tablespoons	1 fl.oz	30 mL
¼ cup	2 fl.oz	60 mL
½ cup	4 fl.oz	120 mL
1 cup	8 fl.oz	240 mL
1½ cup	12 fl.oz	355 mL
2 cups or 1 pint	16 fl.oz	475 mL
4 cups or 1 quart	32 fl.oz	1 L
1 gallon	128 fl.oz	4 L

VOLUME EQUIVALENTS (DRY)

US STANDARD	METRIC (APPROXIMATE)
⅛ teaspoon	0.5 mL
¼ teaspoon	1 mL
½ teaspoon	2 mL
¾ teaspoon	4 mL
1 teaspoon	5 mL
1 tablespoon	15 mL
¼ cup	59 mL
½ cup	118 mL
¾ cup	177 mL
1 cup	235 mL
2 cups	475 mL
3 cups	700 mL
4 cups	1 L

TEMPERATURES EQUIVALENTS

FAHRENHEIT (F)	CELSIUS (C) (APPROXIMATE)
225°F	107°C
250°F	120°C
275°F	135°C
300°F	150°C
325°F	160°C
350°F	180°C
375°F	190°C
400°F	205°C
425°F	220°C
450°F	235°C
475°F	245°C
500°F	260°C

WEIGHT EQUIVALENTS

US STANDARD	METRIC (APPROXIMATE)
1 ounce	28 g
2 ounces	57 g
5 ounces	142 g
10 ounces	284 g
15 ounces	425 g
16 ounces (1 pound)	455 g
1.5 pounds	680 g
2 pounds	907 g

www.ingramcontent.com/pod-product-compliance
Lightning Source LLC
Chambersburg PA
CBHW080610170426
43209CB00007B/1391